The People of
FIFE
1600 - 1799

By
David Dobson

CLEARFIELD

ISBN 9780806358635

INTRODUCTION

The People of Fife 1600-1799

The County of Fife is on the east coast of Scotland and lies between two river estuaries--To the south lies the Firth of Forth and to the north lies the Firth of Tay. During the Dark Ages Fife formed a distinct Pictish kingdom but from the medieval period it has been fully integrated into the kingdom of Scotland. King James VI of Scotland [later King James I of England] described Fife as "a beggar's mantle with a golden fringe" due to the prosperity of the coastal burghs from St Andrews in the east to Kirkcaldy and Dunfermline in the west, with several important fishing villages lying in between.

During the period 1600-1799 the economy of Fife was based on exports of fish, coal, salt, agricultural produce, linen and other textiles. Its seafaring communities were engaged in fishing and whaling, conducting trading voyages to ports in Scandinavia, the Baltic lands, Germany, the Netherlands, France, Spain and the Americas. These shipping links led to emigration in due course. Among such emigrants were John Cunningham, who led a Danish expedition to Greenland and Labrador in 1605, later settling in Norway; General John Forbes, who fought in the French and Indian War and is buried in Philadelphia; and Samuel Greig, 1735-1788, the founder of the Russian Navy. Another notable son of the region was Adam Smith, 1723-1790, philosopher, economist, and author of *The Wealth of Nations*, who was born in Kirkcaldy.

This source book of Fife inhabitants who lived between 1600 and 1799 is based on research into primary source material, both manuscript and printed, largely found in archives in Fife and in Edinburgh.

David Dobson

Dundee, Scotland, 2018.

PEOPLE OF FIFE, 1600-1799

REFERENCES

ABR = Auchtermuchty Burgess Roll

AJ   = Aberdeen Journal

ANY = St Andrew's Society of New York

BA   = Balmerino and its Abbey, [Edinburgh, 1899]

BM = Blackwood's Magazine

BPL = Britain and Poland-Lithuania, [Leiden, 2008]

CBR = Crail Burgess Roll/Cupar Burgess Roll

CLRO   City of London Record Office

CSPAWI Calendar State Papers America & West Indies

DBR = Dundee Burgess Roll

DCA = Dundee City Archives

DCB = Dictionary of Canadian Biography

DM   = Dunfermline Museum

DP = Darien Papers

EA = Edinburgh Advertiser

EEC = Edinburgh Evening Courant

ERA = Edinburgh Register of Apprentices

F = Fasti Ecclesiae Scoticanae

GAR = Rotterdam Archives

GM = Gentleman's Magazine

PEOPLE OF FIFE, 1600-1799

HBRS = Hudson Bay Record Society

HIR = History of Rosyth & Inverkeithing

HL = Hay of Leys pp, University of St Andrews

HSBC = History of Somonauk Presbyterian Church

KBR = Kirkcaldy Burgess Roll

KT = Nederlands Rekeningen in de Tolregisteren van

   En , 1588-1602. ['sGravenhage, 1971]

MAGU Matriculation Album Glasgow University

NARA = National Archives, Records Administration

NBR = Newburgh Burgess Roll

NCSA = North Carolina State Archives

NEHGS = New England Historic Genealogical Society

NJSA = New Jersey State Archives

NLS = National Library of Scotland

NRS = National Records of Scotland, Edinburgh

NWI = New World Immigrants

RGS = Register of the Great Seal of Scotland

RPCS = Register of the Privy Council of Scotland

SAB = Bergen Archives, Norway

SAU = St Andrews University

SABR = St Andrews Burgess Roll

SBRS = Scottish Burgh Record Society

SCHGM = South Carolina Hist. Gen. Magazine

SEC = Scottish Episcopal Clergy

SG = Scottish Genealogist

SHS = Scottish History Society

SIG = Scots in Germany

SM = Scots Magazine

SP = Scots Peerage

SUL = St Andrews University Library

TNA = The National Archives, Kew

ZA = Zealand Archives

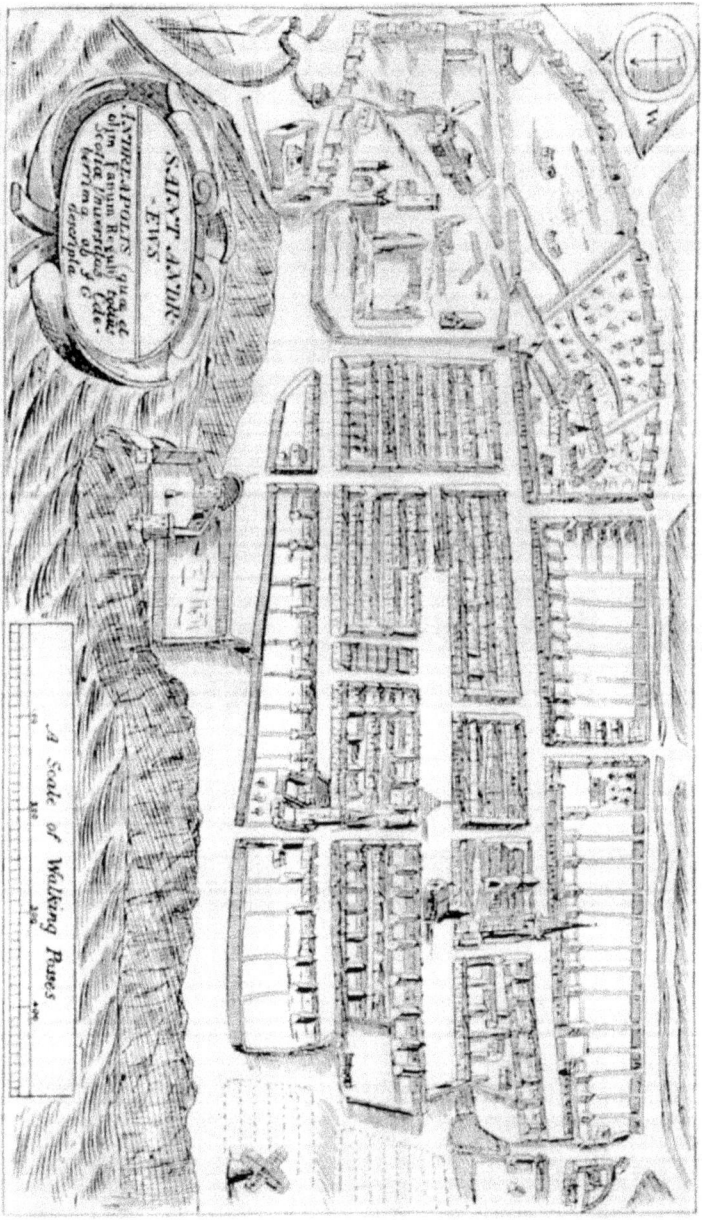

PLAN OF ST. ANDREWS, 1642

PEOPLE OF FIFE, 1600-1799

ABBEY, ARTHUR, a skipper in Crail, testament, 1621, Comm. St Andrews. [NRS]

ABBEY, EDWARD, a mariner burgess of Crail, testament, 1595, Comm. Edinburgh. [NRS]

ABBEY, JOHN, a skipper in Crail, 1635. [RPCS.VI.572]

ABERCROMBIE, ALEXANDER, in Abercrombie, testament, 1615, Comm. St Andrews. [NRS]

ABERCROMBIE, ALEXANDER, son of John Abercrombie a baker burgess of Cupar, a burgess of St Andrews in 1739. [SABR]

ABERCROMBIE, ALEXANDER, a tobacconist in St Andrews, testament, 1742, Comm. St Andrews. [NRS]

ABERCROMBIE, ANN, daughter of John Alexander the younger a baker in Cupar, a deed, 1792. [NRS.B13.7.5/289]

ABERCROMBIE, JAMES, a skipper from Dundee, a burgess of St Andrews in 1727. [SABR]

ABERCROMBIE, JAMES, vintner in Kilconquhar, testaments, 1718, Comm. St Andrews. [NRS]

ABERCROMBIE, JAMES, in Kilconquhar, 1731. [NRS.GD62.325]

ABERCROMBIE, JAMES, a dyer in Kirkcaldy, a deed, 1768 refers to Reverend Robert Abercrombie a minister in Pelham, New England. [NRS.B21.5.2/54]

ABERCROMBIE, JAMES, a merchant from Kilmarnock, a burgess of St Andrews in 1772. [SABR]

ABERCROMBIE, JEAN, relict of Peter Hutton a dyer in Cupar, testament, 1759, Comm. St Andrews. [NRS]

1

ABERCROMBIE, JOHN, a baker and Convenor of the Trades in Cupar. Husband of Ann Paterson, parents of John, Robert, and George, a disposition, 1761. [NRS.B13.7.3.79]

ABERCROMBIE, JOHN, a baker burgess of Cupar, son of the late John Abercrombie a baker in Cupar, father of Ann Abercrombie, a disposition, 1765. [NRS.B13.7.3/124]

ABERCROMBIE, THOMAS, of Abercrombie, testament, 1625, Comm. St Andrews. [NRS]

ABERCROMBIE, WILLIAM, and his wife Janet Horseburgh, in Pittenweem, a deed, 1657. [NRS.GD62.228]

ACHYNDACHY, WILLIAM, a vintner in North Queensferry, testament, 1774, Comm. St Andrews. [NRS]

ADAM, ANDREW, born 1744, son of James Adam and his wife Margaret Petrie, died 1756. [Forgan gravestone]

ADAM, ISOBEL, daughter of Walter Adam a merchant burgess of Burntisland, a deed, 1739. [NRS.B9.11.13]

ADAM, JAMES, with his wife Margaret Rynd, and son William, in Ferryport-on-Craig, a sasine, 1608. [NRS.RS30.XI.118]

ADAM, JAMES, a baker in Markinch, testaments, 1720, Comm. St Andrews. [NRS]

ADAMS, JEAN, daughter of Colin Adams minister at Anstruther Easter, testament, 1692, Comm. St Andrews. [NRS]

ADAM, JOHN, a merchant burgess of Strathmiglo, testament, 1652, Comm. St Andrews. [NRS]

ADAM, MARGARET, daughter of William Adam a skipper in Ferryport on Craig, and relict of James Henryson there, a sasine, 1646. [NRS.RSXV.383]

ADAM, RACHEL, relict of Alexander Pitcairn sometime Principal of New College, University of St Andrews, in Kingsbarns, testament, 1709. [NRS]

ADAM, ROBERT, a tailor burgess of Dunfermline, testament, 1661, Comm. St Andrews. [NRS] NRS.B9.11.13/21]

ADAM, THOMAS, a skipper in Burntisland, a deed of factory in favour of spouse Mary Trotter, 1733, [1749. [NRS.S/H]

ADAM, WALTER, a councillor of Burntisland in 1689. [RPCS.XIV.455]

ADAM, WILLIAM, a skipper in Ferryport on Craig, and his wife Isobel Frisell, sasines, 1643-1646. [NRS.RS31.XIV.265; XV.383]

ADAM, WILLIAM, a merchant and book-seller in Culross, a deed, 1702. [NRS.RD3.98.307]

ADAMSON, AGNES, spouse to Alexander Fairfull the elder, a cordiner burgess of St Andrews, testament, 1620, Comm. St Andrews. [NRS]

ADAMSON, ALEXANDER, in Abercrombie, testament, 1616, Comm. St Andrews. [NRS]

ADAMSON, ALEXANDER, a mariner in St Monance, testament, 1618, Comm. St Andrews. [NRS]

ADAMSON, ALEXANDER, a skipper in Pittenweem, testament, 1625, Comm. St Andrews. [NRS]

ADAMSON, ALEXANDER, a mariner in Pittenweem, husband of Katherine Lundie, sasine 1653, deed 1688, [NRS.RS31.18.244; RD3.68.281]

ADAMSON, ALEXANDER, son of Robert Adamson a mealmaker burgess, a mealmaker burgess of St Andrews in 1738. [SABR]

ADAMSON, ALEXANDER, a maltman burgess of St Andrews, testament, 1755, Comm. St Andrews. [NRS]

ADAMSON, ANDREW, a skipper in St Monance, a sasine, 1628. [NRS.RS30.7.179]

ADAMSON, ANDREW, a mariner in St Andrews, testament, Comm. St Andrews, 1721. [NRS]

ADAMSON, CHARLES, a cooper burgess of Inverkeithing, testament, 1695, Comm. St Andrews. [NRS]

ADAMSON, CHRISTIAN, a writer in St Andrews, a burgess there in 1768. [SABR]

ADAMSON, DAVID, a skipper, husband of Margaret Key, a sasine, 1623. [NRS.RD30.4.345]

ADAMSON, DAVID, in Ferryport on Craig, husband of Isobel Fraser, a sasine, 1651. [NRS.RS31.XVIII.160]

ADAMSON, DAVID, a miller burgess of Kinghorn, testament, 1652, Comm. St Andrews. [NRS]

ADAMSON, DAVID, a hammerman in St Andrews, a bond, 1676, [NRS.RD4.39.635]

ADAMSON, GEORGE, a burgess of Cupar, father of Arthur and Margaret, a disposition, 1721. [NRS.B13.7.2/18]

ADAMSON, GEORGE, eldest son of George Adamson, a blacksmith burgess of St Andrews in 1725. [SABR]

ADAMSON, GRIZEL, spouse to James Dalgleish a skipper burgess of St Andrews, testament, 1648, Comm. St Andrews. [NRS]

ADAMSON, HENRY, in Hilltarvet, Cupar, testament, 1687, Comm. St Andrews. [NRS]

PEOPLE OF FIFE, 1600-1799

ADAMSON, JAMES, in Newburgh, 1760, took the Oath of Allegiance in 1761. [NRS.B54.7.3]

ADAMSON, JAMES, a brewer burgess of Newburgh, 1748. [NRS.B54.7.3]

ADAMSON, JOHN, a cordiner at Kirkton of Largo, testament, 1650, Comm. St Andrews. [NRS]

ADAMSON, JOHN, a skipper in Crail 1692, master of the John of Crail in 1669, [NRS.E72.9.17; E72.7.4]; testament, 1718, Comm. St Andrews. [NRS]; husband of Euphan Corsar [1682-1765], father of John Adamson [1718-]. [NLS.3474/233][Crail gravestone]

ADAMSON, JOHN, master of the Charles of Crail trading with St Sebastian in Spain in 1726. [NRS.CE52.1.3]

ADAMSON, JOHN, a baker in Newburgh, 1784. [NRS.B54.1.1]

ADAMSON, JOHN, a skipper in Pittenweem, master of the Euphan of Pittenweem in 1772, manager of the Pittenweem Sea Box Society in 1787. [NRS.B3.7.5; E504.24.8]

ADAMSON, LAURENCE, born 1766, son of John Adamson and his wife Sophia Key, died in April 1789 in Bengal. [St Andrews gravestone]

ADAMSON, MICHAEL, a burgess of Newburgh in 1678. [HL.350]

ADAMSON, WILLIAM, a skipper in Crail, master of the Elizabeth of Crail in 1666, master of the Janet of Crail in 1670, master of the Content of Crail in 1681, and master of the William of Crail in 1683, deeds, [NRS.RD3.9.583; RD2.57.316; RD4.52.34; E72.9.4/10/14]; testament, 1691, Comm. St Andrews. [NRS]

ADIE, DAVID, a writer in Dunfermline, 1752. [NRS.CS16.1.88]

AFFLECK, JOHN, born 1670, minister at Auchterderran from 1700 until his death in Edinburgh on 22 May 1740. [F.V.77]

AIKEN, DAVID, was admitted as a weaver burgess of Cupar on 16 February 1759. [CBR]

AIKEN, HENRY, born 1694, a sailor in Aberdour, foremastman aboard the Gilbert bound from Gravesend, Kent, to Maryland in December 1717. [TNA.HCA.Lowry versus Whale, 1719]

AIKEN, JAMES, a meal-maker in St Andrews, a bond, 1696. [NRS.B65.5.1/105]

AIKEN, JOHN, master of the Jamieson and Peggy of Kinghorn trading with Boston and with Charleston in 1765, 1772, 1773. [South Carolina Gazette][NRS.E504.20.8/12]

AIKENHEAD, PATRICK, son of David Aikenhead the Customs Surveyor of Anstruther, a burgess of St Andrews, 1728. [SABR]

AIKMAN, ALEXANDER, son of Thomas Aikman, a mealmaker, was admitted as a burgess of St Andrews on 21 April 1759.[SABR]

AIRTH, DAVID, a merchant burgess of Cupar, testament, 1620, Comm. St Andrews. [NRS]

AITCHISON, JOHN, master of the Sun of Pittenweem trading with Rotterdam in 1681. [NRS.E72.9.10]; master of the Anna of Pittenweem trading between Rotterdam and Leith in 1707. [NRS.GD29.427]

AITCHISON, JOHN, a bailie of Pittenweem, a deed, 1702. [NRS.RD2.86.463]

AITKEN, AGNES, relict of James Wilson a tanner in Cupar, a disposition in 1788. [NRS.B13.7.5/345]

AITKEN, ALEXANDER, a mariner and a baillie of St Andrews, relict Elizabeth Yooll, a bond, 1697. [NRS.B65.5.1/117]

AITKEN, DAVID, a burgess of Cupar, and spouse Janet Geddy, a bond, 1671. [NRS.RD2.29.272]

AITKEN, DAVID, a mariner aboard HMS Solebay a letter of attorney to his wife Janet Masterton in Low Valleyfield, 1759. [NRS.B20.6.5/176]

AITKEN, HENRY, from Kinghorn, a member of the Scots Charitable Society of Boston, Massachusetts, in 1740. [NEHGS]

AITKEN, JOHN, son of Andrew Aitken a mariner in Linktown, was apprenticed to David Fife a tailor in Linktown of Abbotshall for 4 years in 1701. [NRS.RH11.27.30/57]

AITKEN, JOHN, a sailor in Kinghorn, a deed, 1750. [NRS.RD3.210.571]

AITKEN, MARGARET, spouse of Charles French a wright in Dunfermline, a deed, 1702. [NRS.RD4.91.545]

AITKEN, ROBERT, born 1793, a Captain of the 6th Bengal Cavalry, died on 21 December 1852. [Cupar gravestone]

AITKEN, WILLIAM, a merchant and a baillie of Falkland, a deed, 1749. [NRS.GD1.392.166]

AITKEN, WILLIAM, eldest son of James Aitken a shoemaker in St Andrews, was admitted as a burgess of St Andrews on 30 November 1759. [SABR]

AITKEN, WILLIAM, in St Andrews, 1798. [NRS.E326.15.31]

ALBURN, ANDREW, a mariner aboard the Pincher of Burntisland a gunboat, testament, 1802, Comm. St Andrews. [NRS]

ALEXANDER, DAVID, a weaver burgess of Newburgh in 1777. [NRS.B54.7.3]

ALEXANDER, GEORGE, a Covenanter in Newburgh, banished to the American Plantations in 1678, transported from Leith aboard the St Michael of Scarborough bound for Jamaica in 1678. [RPCS.VI.76]

ALEXANDER, GEORGE, a fisherman in Kilrenny, 1702. [NRS.GD26.12.16]

ALEXANDER, JAMES, a mariner in Scoonie, testament, 1619, Comm. St Andrews. [NRS]

ALEXANDER, JAMES, a skipper in Inverkeithing, 1798. [NRS.S/H]

ALEXANDER, JOHN, a carpenter in Burntisland, a deed of factory in favour of his wife Helen Ritchie, 1736. [NRS.B9.11.13/98]

ALEXANDER, JOHN, a mariner in Burntisland, testament, 1694, Comm. St Andrews. [NRS]

ALEXANDER, JOHN, a brewer in Aberdour, 1795. [NRS.CS230.SEQNS.A1.12]

ALEXANDER, JOHN, a skipper in Inverkeithing, testament, 1804, Comm. St Andrews. [NRS]

ALEXANDER, PHILIP, in St Andrews, deeds, 1683. [NRS.RD3.57.45; RD4.52.254]

ALISON, ANDREW, in Ferryport on Craig, 1762. [NRS.CH2.150.4.29]

ALISON, DAVID, a mariner in Dysart, testament, 1629, Comm. St Andrews. [NRS]

ALISON, JAMES, was served heir to his father Nicol Alison a smith in Cupar on 27 June 1752. [NRS.S/H]; was admitted as a hammerman burgess of Cupar on 28 September 1767. [CBR]

ALISON, JOHN, schoolmaster of Leslie in 1690. [SHS.4.2]

ALISON, JOHN, was admitted as a burgess of St Andrews on 23 January 1759. [SABR]

ALISON, JOHN, son of Simon Alison a weaver in St Andrews, was admitted as a burgess of St Andrews on12 August 1774. [SABR]

ALLAN, DAVID, a skipper in St Andrews, testament, 1636, Comm. St Andrews. [NRS]

ALLAN, DAVID, was admitted as a merchant burgess and guilds-brother of Cupar on 5 September 1785, [CBR]; a tack, 1787. [NRS.B13.7.5/192]

ALLEN, GEORGE, from Fife, a member of the Scots Charitable Society of Boston, Massachusetts, in 1736. [NEHGS]

ALLAN, JAMES, a mariner in St Andrews, son of Reverend Andrew Allan in Leuchars, 1645. [NRS.S/H]

ALLAN, JAMES, a burgess of Newburgh in 1698. [HL.338]

ALLAN, JAMES, from Dysart, was admitted as a citizen of Rotterdam on 31 May 1777. [GAR]

ALLAN, JOHN, in Newburgh, 1612. [HL.320]

ALLAN, JOHN, a schoolmaster from Kirkcaldy, settled in Nevis before 1783. [NRS.CS17.1.2]

ALLAN, THOMAS, a meal-maker in Kilmaron, Cupar, testament, 1635, Comm. St Andrews. [NRS]

ALLAN, WILLIAM, a skipper in Leven, testament, 1773, Comm. Edinburgh. [NRS]; master of the Friendship of Leven trading with Hamburg in 1767. [NRS.E504.3.3]

ALLARDYCE, JOHN, a burgess of St Andrews, a deed, 1687. [NRS.RD2.68.1608]

ALLOWAY, ALEXANDER, in Balmerino, 1653. [RGS.X.106]

ALLOWAY, THOMAS, in Balmerino, 1653. [RGS.X.106]

ALVIE, JOHN, in Newburgh, 1657. [RGS.X.622]

AMBROSE, JOSEPH, a tailor burgess of Newburgh in 1747. [NRS.B54.7.3]

AMBROSE, WALTER, a cooper burgess of Newburgh in 1790. [NRS.B54.7.3]

ANDERSON, ALEXANDER, a maltman in Cupar, deeds, 1669. [NRS.RD423.62; RD4.24.151]

ANDERSON, ALEXANDER, manager of the Pittenweem Sea Box Society, 1708. [NRS.B3.7.4]; a skipper in Pittenweem, 1719. [NRS.B3.7.4]

ANDERSON, ALEXANDER, tenant in Seggie, was admitted as a burgess of St Andrews on 4 June 1770. [SABR]

ANDERSON, ANDREW, born 1761, feuar of Bottom Craig, died 1837. [Balmerino gravestone]

ANDERSON, ANDREW, a tenant in Brownhills, a tack, 1762. [NRS.B65.5.5/80]

ANDERSON, ANN, born 1792, daughter of Laurence Anderson and his wife Jane Watson, died in New York on 24 November 1825. [St Andrews gravestone]

ANDERSON, ANNIE, born 21 March 1786 in Newburgh, died at the Cape of Good Hope in 1813. [Abdie gravestone]

ANDERSON, BESSIE, spouse to John Dais in Cupar, testament, 1596, Comm. St Andrews. [NRS]

ANDERSON, CHRISTIAN, spouse to John Christison a burgess of Cupar, a testament, 1640, Comm. St Andrews. [NRS]

ANDERSON, DAVID, town clerk of Cupar, testament, 1698, Comm. St Andrews. [NRS]

ANDERSON, ELSPETH, daughter of the late Alexander Anderson the younger, a burgess of Cupar, a dispensation, 1764. [NRS.B13.7.3/158]

ANDERSON, FLETCHER, son of George Anderson an inn-keeper in Cupar, was apprenticed to Alexander Ferguson a watch and clock maker in Cupar, in 1762. [NRS.B13,7.3/163]

ANDERSON, GEORGE, a merchant in Cupar, husband of Isabel Philp, parents of Isobel, deed, 1682, 1688. [NRS.RD2.57.523; AC7.9]

ANDERSON, GEORGE, of Foxtoun, Cupar, testament, 1690, Comm. St Andrews. [NRS]

ANDERSON, GEORGE, an inn-keeper in Cupar, a deed, 1770. [NRS.B13.7.3.343]

ANDERSON, JAMES, a waulker at Cook's Milne, Cupar, testament, 1614, Comm. St Andrews. [NRS]

ANDERSON, JAMES, the elder, a maltman in Cupar, testament, 1626, Comm. St Andrews. [NRS]

ANDERSON, JAMES, a maltman of Cupar, testament, 1653, Comm. St Andrews. [NRS]

ANDERSON, JAMES, a shoemaker in Cupar, relict Elspeth Gardener, deeds, 1687. [NRS.RD4.69.765; RD4.60.160]

ANDERSON, JAMES, a smith burgess of Dunfermline, and Christian Wilson, daughter of John Wilson a weaver in Dunfermline, a marriage contract, 1753. [NRS.B20.6.8/17]

ANDERSON, JAMES, born 1797, son of Laurence Anderson and his wife Jane Watson, died in Newark, USA, on 12 April 1830. [St Andrews gravestone]

ANDERSON, JANET, born 1718, wife of John Melvill a smith, died 16 February 1791. [Culross Abbey gravestone]

ANDERSON, JOHN, the younger, in Kinloch, Collessie, 1658. [RGS.X.671]

ANDERSON, JOHN, a Notary Public in Cupar, bonds, 1666-1669. [NRS.RD4.15.499; RD2.24.354]

ANDERSON, JOHN, from Dunfermline, settled in Danbury, Connecticut, probate 6 March 1740, Connecticut.

ANDERSON, JOHN, a farmer in Kirkcaldy, was served heir to his mother Agnes Paton, wife of Thomas Anderson in Dunnikier, on 6 January 1753. [NRS.S/H]

ANDERSON, JOHN, a merchant in Cupar, a deed, 1689. [NRS.RD2.69.552]

ANDERSON, JOHN, a Customs Officer, was admitted as a burgess of St Andrews on 4 June 1770. [SABR]

ANDERSON, JOHN, born 1790, son of James Anderson, died in Halifax, North America, on 17 July 1810. [Kilrenny gravestone]

ANDERSON, JOHN, born 2 October 1796 in Newburgh, a minister who died in Nice on 16 March 1834. [Newburgh gravestone]

ANDERSON, MARGARET, in Auchtermuchtie, and Thomas Gray, a process of declarator of marriage, 3 March 1797. [NRS.CC8.6.62]

ANDERSON, MARION, relict of Captain James Duncan a merchant in Kirkcaldy, a deed, 1752. [NRS.RD9.11.13/383]

ANDERSON, MATTHEW, a maltman in Linkton of Abbotshall, husband of Janet Cunningham, a deed, 1702. [NRS.RD3.98.628]

ANDERSON, PETER, a merchant in Cupar, a deed, 1689. [NRS.RD2.69.552]

ANDERSON, ROBERT, a merchant in Dunfermline, and Elisabeth Mastertoun, a post nuptial marriage contract, 1707. [NRS.RH11.27.36/114]

ANDERSON, THOMAS, a merchant in Gothenburg, Sweden, was admitted as burgess of St Andrews in 1728. [SABR]

ANDERSON, WILLIAM, from Dunfermline, settled in Deerfield, Massachusetts in 1758, married Abigail Hitchcock, died 1810. [Imm.NE.1700-1775]

ANDERSON, WILLIAM, a weaver, eldest son of Robert Anderson a weaver in St Andrews, was admitted as a burgess of St Andrews on 31 January 1757. [SABR]

ANDERSON, WILLIAM, a wigmaker, was admitted as a burgess of St Andrews on 6 August 1765. [SABR]

ANDREW, JAMES, the elder, a wright in Cupar, husband of Janet Donaldson, a deed, 1686. [NRS.RD2.65.791]

ANDREW, JAMES, the younger, a wright in Cupar, husband of Margaret Bousie, a deed, 1686. [NRS.RD2.65.791]

ANGUS, JOHN, a councillor of Burntisland in 1689. [RPCS.XIV.455]

ANGUS, JOHN, a merchant in London, eldest son and heir of John Angus a mariner in Burntisland, and grandson of John Angus a mariner in Burntisland, letters of attorney in favour of Robert Angus a mariner in Leith, 1738. [NRS.B9.11.13/162]

ANGUS, PATRICK, a mariner in Kinghorn, born 1704, a bailie of Burntisland, died 4 December 1741, father of Patrick, born 1739, died 12 August 1741. [Burntisland, St Columba's, gravestone]

ANGUS, WILLIAM, servant to Dr Forrest, was admitted as a burgess of St Andrews in 1774. [SABR]

ANNAL, DAVID, a weaver, third son of William Annal in St Andrews, was admitted as a burgess of St Andrews on 12 August 1774. [SABR]

ANNAN, DAVID, born 1754 in Cupar, son of John Annan, married Mary Smith, settled in Peterborough, New Hampshire, died 1802 in Ireland. [INE.5]

ANNAN, JOHN, a writer in Cupar, testament, 1781, Comm. St Andrews. [NRS]

ANSTRUTHER, ANNE, wife of Captain Philip Anstruther of Inverkeithing, was served heir to her father John Landale of Airdit, on 9 June 1757. [NRS.S/H]

ANSTRUTHER, CHARLES, son of Sir Philip Anstruther of Balcaskie, died in Dominica on 26 January 1778. [Ruddiman's Weekly Mercury.22]

ANSTRUTHER, ROBERT, was admitted as a burgess of St Andrews on 4 October 1768. [SABR]

ANSTRUTHER, Sir WILLIAM, of Anstruther, probate 1653, Prerogative Court of Canterbury. [TNA]

ARBUTHNOTT, JAMES, graduated MA from St Andrews in 1674, Episcopalian minister of Dysart from 1685 to 1689, later a skipper, husband of Christian Boswell. [SEC.7]

ARCHIBALD, JOHN, a candle-maker in Elie, and his wife Helen Elder, a deed, 1757. [NRS.GD1.27.47]

ARCHIBALD, WILLIAM, from Kirkcaldy, a musketeer aboard the Vere in 1644. [Zeeuws Archief]

ARNOT, ALEXANDER, a mariner in Kinghorn, testament, 1719, Comm. Edinburgh. [NRS].

ARNOT, ALEXANDER, a smith in Aberdour, brother of late Captain Thomas Arnot in Rotterdam, and Isobel Moyes, a deed, 1782. [NRS.B9.7.2/399]

ARNOTT, DAVID, son of David Arnott a mealmaker burgess, was admitted as a burgess of St Andrews on 11 September 1761 [SABR]

ARNOT, JAMES, son of Peter Arnot of Balcormo, a goldsmith in Schillez, Danzig, before 1605. [NRS.RS31.5.86]

ARNOT, JAMES, a councillor of Auchtermuchty, 1784. [NRS.CS228.A5.23]

ARNOTT, JOHN, son of David Arnott a guilds-brother, was admitted as a burgess of St Andrews on 21 September 1764. [SABR]

ARNOT, MARGARET, relict of Simon Gregor a burgess of Cupar, testament, 1600, Comm. St Andrews. [NRS]

ARNOT, ROBERT, schoolmaster of Falkland in 1683. [NRS.RD4.52.750]

ARNOTT, ROBERT, and his wife Sarah Walker in Auchtertool, a deed, 1687. [NRS.GD1.49.37]

ARNOT, THOMAS, graduated MA from St Andrews University in 1646, minister at Cupar from 1658 until his death in 1694, husband of Eupham Inglis. [F.V.143]

ARNOT, THOMAS, a mariner from Largo, died at sea aboard the Olepius, probate 1673, Prerogative Court of Canterbury. [TNA]

ARNOT, THOMAS, master of the Two Brothers of Aberdour bound for Philadelphia in 1747. [NRS.E504.28.1]

ARNOT, WILLIAM, son of Peter Arnot of Balcormo, a goldsmith in Schillez, Danzig, before 1605. [NRS.RS31.5.86]

ARNOT, WILLIAM, a baillie of Falkland, was admitted as a maltman burgess of Auchtermuchty on 5 December 1742. [ABR]

ARNOT, WILLIAM, son of Thomas Arnot in Fife, probate 17 November 1790, Charleston, South Carolina.

ARTHUR, WILLIAM, born 1639 in Crail, foremast-man aboard the Edward bound from London to Virginia in 1669. [TNA.HCA.VOL.74: September 1669]

ATKIN, GEORGE, from Kirkcaldy, a member of the Scots Charitable Society of Boston, New England, 1730. [NEHGS]

ATKIN, HENRY, from Kinghorn, a member of the Scots Charitable Society of Boston in 1740. [NEHGS]

AUCHENLECK, ALEXANDER, son of Andrew Auchenleck and his wife Janet Lindsay in Dundee, graduated MA from St Andrews in 1660, Episcopalian minister of Dunbog from 1666 to 1689. [SEC.7]

AUCHENLECK, ANDREW, born 1640, graduated MA from St Andrews in 1665, Episcopalian minister of Dunino from 1672 to 1682, died in August 1696. [SEC.7]

AUCHENLECK, JOHN, born 1628, son of Andrew Auchenleck and his wife Janet Lindsay in Dundee, Episcopalian minister of Largo from 1665 to 1689. [SEC.7]

AUCHINLECK, THOMAS, born 1655, graduated MA from St Andrews in 1682, Episcopalian minister of Anstruther Wester in 1689. [SEC.8]

AUCHMUTIE, ROBERT, Commendator of Balmerino, a sasine, 1609. [NRS.RS30.XI.194]

AULD, JANET, relict of Alexander Masterton the clerk of Dysart, a deed, 1696. [NRS.B21.5.1/11]

AYTON, DAVID, a mariner in Kirkcaldy, testament, 1654, Comm. St Andrews. [NRS]

AYTON, JAMES, [formerly Monypenny], of Kinnaldie, son of D. Monipenny of Pitmillie, was served heir to Captain Alexander Ayton of Kinnaldie on 9 February 1758. [NRS.S/H]

AYTON, RACHEL, widow of James Graham a carpenter in Burntisland, a deed, 1748. [NRS.B9.11.13/343]

BAIN, ALEXANDER, a cooper in Burntisland, a bond, 1737. [NRS.B9.8.1/115]

BAIN, JAMES, a dancing master, was admitted as a burgess of St Andrews on 18 April 1757. [SABR]

BAIN, JOHN, a type-founder in St Andrews in 1742, later in Philadelphia. [SSA.86]

BAIRD, ALEXANDER, master of the James and Elizabeth of Kirkcaldy trading with Rotterdam in 1722. [NRS.CE52.1.3]

BAIRD, ELIZABETH, wife of John Boswell a glazier in Kirkcaldy, was served her to her grandfather James Brymer a merchant there on 31 October 1750. [NRS.S/H]

BAIRD, JAMES, a shipmaster from Kirkcaldy, an assessor of the Scots Court at Veere, Zeeland, in 1728. [NRS.RH11/2]

BAIRD, PATRICK, late of Philadelphia, was admitted as a burgess of St Andrews on 2 October 1759. [SABR]

BAIRD, WILLIAM, born 1689 in Kirkcaldy, a sailor aboard the Alexander bound for Maryland in 1710. [TNA.HCA.84]

BALCANQUELL, JAMES, of that Ilk, residing in Cupar, testament, 1786, Comm. St Andrews. [NRS]

BALCANQUELL, JOHN, master of the Daniel of Kirkcaldy trading with the Netherlands in 1627. [RPCS.VII.440]

BALCAM, JAMES, a mealmaker in Burntisland, a bond, 1740. [NRS.B9.11.13/257]

BALCOMIE, DAVID, schoolmaster of Cupar in 1619, son of Thomas Balcomie a burgess of Cupar, husband of Janet Gregor, parents of Katherine, Jane, and Margaret. [NRS.RS30.2.254]

BALD, DAVID, master of the privateer Hopewell of Crail in 1627. [RPCS.2.20]

BALDIE, ROBERT, Convenor of the Trades in Cupar, husband of Jean Smith, testament, 1757, Comm. St Andrews. [NRS]

BALDIE, ROBERT, in Cupar, was admitted as a burgess of St Andrews in 1774. [SABR]

BALDIE, ROBERT, clerk to John Finlayson a writer in Cupar, only son of Robert Baldie the younger, a glover in Cupar, a deed, 1796. [NRS.B13.7,5331]

BALFOUR, ALEXANDER, a burgess of Cupar, a deed, 1671. [NRS.RD4.29.769]

BALFOUR, DAVID, born 1751, died 15 June 1796, husband of Janet Braid, born 1774, died in August 1821. [Carnock gravestone]

BALFOUR, HENRY, of Halbeath, graduated MA from St Andrews in 1677, Episcopalian minister at Auchtertool from 1686 to 1693. [F.V.78][SEC.9]

BALFOUR, Major HENRY, of Dunbog, son of John Balfour the Earl of Burleigh, a Jacobite who was imprisoned in Carlisle in December 1716. [SAU.Cheap ms5.537]

BALFOUR, JAMES, of Radernie, and Ann, daughter of David Balfour of Grange, a marriage contract, 1703. [NRS.GD1.361.1/241]

BALFOUR, Colonel JOHN, of Fernie, a Jacobite who was imprisoned in Carlisle in 1716. [SAU.Cheap ms5.537]

BALFOUR, JOHN, of Dunbog, was admitted as a burgess of St Andrews on 4 June 1761. [SABR]

BALFOUR, JOHN, in Tobago, eldest son of John Balfour Crawford of Powmiln and Elizabeth Maxwell, a deed, 1778. [NRS.RD4.775/1.175]

BALFOUR, MICHAEL, in Kingask, Cupar, testament, 1637, Comm. St Andrews. [NRS]

BALFOUR, MICHAEL, of Forret, Logie, a Jacobite in 1715. [NRS.E672]

BALFOUR, MITCHELL, master of the Mayflower of Pittenweem in 1602. [RPCS.6.758]

BALFOUR, Sir MICHAEL, of Denmylne, born 1581, died 4 February 1652. [Abdie gravestone]

BALFOUR, ROBERT, son of Duncan Balfour, a wright in Elie, a sasine, 1671. [NRS.GD1.27.10]

BALFOUR, ROBERT, an apothecary in St Andrews, a deed, 1707. [NRS.RD3.114.375]

BALFOUR, THOMAS, a surgeon in Auchtermuchtie, 1752. [NRS.CS228.B42]

BALFOUR, WILLIAM, master of the David of Kirkcaldy trading with Holland in 1672. [NRS.E72.9.5]

BALLANTINE, DAVID, a skipper in Burntisland, spouse Betty Mitchell, a deed, 1746. [NRS.B9.11.13/302]

BALLANTINE, DAVID, born 1753, son of David Ballantine and his wife Elisabeth Mitchell, died in Kingston, Jamaica, on 4 June 1777. [Burntisland gravestone]

BALLENTINE, JAMES, master of the Sophia of Anstruther trding with Gothenburg in 1741. [NRS.E504.27.1]

BALLENTINE, JAMES, master of the Two Brothers of Kirkcaldy bound for Madeira and South Carolina in 1766. [TNA.CO5.511]

BALLANTYNE, Captain, master of the Favorite of Kirkcaldy from Ullapool to Pictou, Nova Scotia, with passengers in 1803. [CNSHS.23.44]

BALLARDIE, THOMAS, master of the Jane and Mary of Kinghorn trading with Norway in 1750. [NRS.E504.3.2]

BALLARDIE, THOMAS, from Anstruther, a master mariner in the Royal Navy, testament, 1809, Comm. St Andrews. [NRS]

BALLINGALL, GEORGE, was admitted as a weaver burgess of Cupar on 14 September 1760. [CBR]

BALLINGALL, ISABEL, born 1697, wife of William Masterton a smith in Valleyfield, died 21 January 1752. [Culross Abbey gravestone]

BALLINGALL, JOHN, a meal-maker in St Andrews, was admitted as a burgess of St Andrews on 30 December 1765. [SABR]

BALLINGALL, THOMAS, was admitted as a burgess of St Andrews in 1774. [SABR]

BALMANNO, DAVID, master of the Mansfield of Crail trading with Gothenburg, Sweden, Rotterdam in the Netherlands, and Christiansund in Norway, 1762-1763; master of the Swift of Crail trading with Veere, Danzig, and Memel in 1767-1768. [NRS.E504.3.3/4]

BALMANNO, JOHN, servant to James Carstairs a tailor in St Andrews, a bond, 1692. [NRS.B65.5.1/18]

BALMAYNE, THOMAS, a mariner in Kirkcaldy, his relict Margaret Greive, a deed, 1675. [NRS.RD3.38.278]

BALVAIRD, ANDREW, a dyer in Dunikier, a tack, 1778. [NRS.B21.5.2/292]

BALVAIRD, JAMES, master of the James of Kirkcaldy trading with London, Holland, Norway, Ostend, and Aberdeen, 1669-1673. [NRS.E72.9.4/5/8]

BALVAIRD, WALTER, a skipper in Kirkcaldy, husband of Margaret Blyth, deeds, 1678/1680/1692. [NRS.RD4.42.726; RD2.51.194; RD4.71.683]

BAND, CHRISTIAN, relict of James Fairnet a maltman in St Andrews, a tack, 1720. [NRS.CC20.13.2]

BAND, JOHN, the elder, a maltman in St Andrews, a bond, 1697. [NRS.B65.5.1/117]

BANKHEAD, WILLIAM, was admitted as a burgess of St Andrews on 21 September 1762. [SABR]

BARBER, JOHN, a fisherman in Buckhaven, 1706. [NRS.GD26.15.21]

BARCLAY, AEMELIA, daughter of David Barclay in Kelty. Was served co-heir to her brother James Barclay, a merchant in Jamaica, on 14 July 1750. [NRS.S/H]

BARCLAY, ALEXANDER, late merchant in Cupar, then in Abbotshall, husband of Elizabeth Balfour, testament, 31 December 1770. Comm. St Andrews. [NRS]

BARCLAY, ALISON, widow of Andrew Hoy a farmer in Beath, was served co-heir to her brother James Barclay a merchant in Jamaica on 14 July 1750. [NRS.S/H]

BARCLAY, ANTONIA, in Lindores, 1717. [NRS.CS226.1244]

BARCLAY, BEATRIX, wife of Andrew Houton in Kelty, was served co-heir to her brother James Barclay, a merchant in Jamaica, on 14 July 1750. [NRS.S/H]

BARCLAY, CHARLES, born 1790, son of Reverend Peter Barclay and his wife Margaret Duddingston in Kettle, died in Guadaloupe in 1819. [F.5.160]

BARCLAY, DAVID, a maltman burgess of Cupar, testament, 1628, Comm. St Andrews. [NRS]

BARCLAY, Sir DAVID, of Cullairny, husband of Helen Aytoun, a bond, 1639. [NRS.GD7.SEC1/44]

BARCLAY, DAVID, born 1649, son of Reverend William Barclay and his wife Annas Arnot in Falkland, graduated MA from St Andrews in 1671, Episcopalian minister at Strathmiglo from 1685 to 1689, died 11 March 1702. [SEC.11]

BARCLAY, ELIZABETH CLELLAND, born 12 February 1792, daughter of Reverend Peter Barclay and his wife Margaret Duddingston in Kettle, wife of Thomas Martin a merchant in Antigua, died 4 December 1841. [F.5.160]

BARCLAY, GEORGE, master of the Maria of Pittenweem trading with Stockholm in 1669. [NRS.E72.7.4]

BARCLAY, GEORGE, master of the Concord of Burntisland bound for St Petersburg, Russia, in 1750. [NRS.E504.24.2]

BARCLAY, GEORGE, master of the Bachelor of Dysart bound for North Carolina in 1775, and bound for Grenada in 1776. [NRS.E504.22.19/20]

BARCLAY, HUGH, was admitted as a wright burgess of Cupar on 10 September 1767. [CBR]

BARCLAY, JAMES, in Kelty, and Anna Thomson, daughter of John Thomson a portioner of Sandidub, a marriage contract. 1714. [NRS.RH11.27.32/223]

BARCLAY, JANET, wife of George Henderson a gardener in Kirkland, was served co-heir to her brother James Barclay a merchant in Jamaica, on 14 June 1750. [NRS.S/H]

BARCLAY, JOHN, a bailie of Cupar, an interdiction, 1672. [NRS.RD3.32.165]

BARCLAY, JOHN, born 1629, son of Reverend William Barclay in Falkland, graduated MA from Glasgow University in 1649, Episcopalian minister of Dunino from 1664 to 1667, and Kettle from 1667 to 1689, died in Edinburgh in July 1691. [SEC.11]

BARCLAY, JOHN, a merchant in Cupar, was admitted as a burgess of St Andrews on 15 April 1762. [SABR]

BARCLAY, JOHN, born 9 July 1795 in Kettle, son of Reverend Peter Barclay and his wife Margaret Duddingston, a minister, educated at Edinburgh University, settled in Kingston, Ontario, died 29 September 1826. [F.5.160]

BARCLAY, ROBERT, son of John Barclay, was admitted as a weaver burgess of Cupar on 29 September 1795. [CBR]

BARCLAY, THOMAS, a maltman burgess of Cupar, testaments, 1617, Comm. St Andrews. [NRS]

BARCLAY, THOMAS, a merchant in St Andrews, spouse of Catherine Lindsay, a sasine, 1659. [NRS.RS30.22.100]

BARDNER, HENRY, a writer in Dunfermline, a deed, 1813. [NRS.B20.7.1/49]

BARKER, GEORGE, master of the Martha and Mary of Kirkcaldy trading with Christiansand in Norway in 1754. [NRS.E504.27.3]

BARRON, ARCHIBALD, a vintner in Falkland, a letter, 1755. [NRS.GD1.392.194]

BARRON, WILLIAM, born 30 November 1735, Professor of Rhetoric and Belle Lettres, died 28 July in 1803, husband of Margaret Stark. [St Andrews gravestone]

BATHGATE, JAMES, minister of Dalgetty, husband of Euphan Anderson, born 1713, died 8 July 1755. [Dalgetty gravestone]

BATHGATE, JAMES, minister at Dalgetty, was served heir to his mother Margaret Gray, wife of James Bathgate minister at Orwell, on 9 January 1754. [NRS.S/H]

BAXTER, DAVID, a burgess of Cupar, deeds, 1670, 1690. [NRS.RD4.24.567; RD2.72.434]

BAXTER, DAVID, a hatter in Kirkcaldy, was admitted as a burgess of St Andrews on 14 January 1766. [SABR]

BAXTER, HENRY, a baker burgess of Cupar, testament, 1648, Comm. St Andrews. [NRS]

BAXTER, JOHN, a burgess of Cupar, an interdiction, 1672. [NRS.RD3.32.165]

BAXTER, JOHN, Provost of Cupar, was admitted as a burgess of St Andrews on 23 November 1765. [SABR]

BAYNE, DAVID, born 1651, son of Alexander Bayne the Sheriff-Clerk if Edinburgh, graduated MA from Edinburgh University in 1671, Episcopalian minister of Moonzie pre 1675 to 1678 , of Kinglassie from 1678 to 1690, died in February 1710. [SEC.12]

BAYNE, JOHN, a merchant in Cupar, husband of Mary Wilson, a disposition, 1717. [NRS.B13.7.2/2]

BAYNE, JOHN, in Cupar, the Sheriff Clerk of Fife, testament, 16 October 1723, Comm. St Andrews. [NRS]

BAYNE, WILLIAM, servant to Sir John Anstruther of that Ilk, was admitted as a burgess of St Andrews on 5 October 1756. [SABR]

BEALL, NINIAN, born in Largo around 1625, a prisoner of war transported to Barbados in 1650, settled in Maryland, died at Fife's Largo, Maryland, in 1717, probate 28 February 1717, Maryland.

BEANS, JAMES, a burgess of St Andrews, a bond, 1709. [NRS.B65.5.2/64]

BEATH, WILLIAM, of Pitgorno, was admitted as a burgess of Auchtermuchty on 5 May 1738. [ABR]

BEAT, JAMES, master of the Alexander and James of Anstruther trading with Hamburg in 1755. [NRS.E504.3.3]

BEAT, WILLIAM, master of the London Packet of Leven trading with Rotterdam in 1744. [NRS.E504.27.1]

BEATON, JAMES, of Blebo the younger, son of John Beaton, and Margaret Wemyss, daughter of James Wemyss of Bogie and his wife Anna Aytoun, a marriage contract, 1696. [NRS.GD7.SEC1.58]

BEATON, JOHN, an apothecary in Cupar, a deed, 1688. [NRS.RD4.63.474]

BEATON, PATRICK, an apothecary in St Andrews, a deed, 1697. [NRS.RD2.80/2.178]

BEATSON, ALEXANDER, a mariner in Burntisland, a deed, 1734. [NRS.B9.11.13/37]

BEATSON, DAVID, of Powguild, Auchterderran, a bond, 1683.

BEATSON, JAMES, of Balbairdie, a deed, 1777. [NRS.B9.7.2/310]

BELL, ALEXANDER, born 1649 in St Andrews, son of Alexander Bell and his wife Margaret Ramsay, died 1744 in Maryland. [SG.28.4.189]

BELL, ANDREW, son of Robert Bell a weaver in St Andrews, was admitted as a burgess of St Andrews on 22 July 1760. [SABR]

BELL, ANDREW, born 27 March 1753 in St Andrews, son of Alexander Bell and his wife Margaret Robertson, educated at St Andrews, a minister and a teacher, a tutor in Virginia in 1774, later a chaplain of the Honorable East India Company Service in Madras, died 27 January 1832. [Westminster Abbey monumental inscription]

BELL, CATHERINE, widow of William Walker a Deacon of the Bakers of St Andrews, a marriage contract, 1712. [NRS.B65.5.2/164]

BELL, CHARLES, late Governor of Annamabee in Africa, a sasine, 1788. [NRS.RS31.1989]

BELL, DAVID, Dean of Guild of Cupar, a deed, 1697. [NRS.RD4.80.1446]

BELL, GEORGE, eldest son of William Bell a guilds-brother of St Andrews, was admitted as a burgess of St Andrews on 6 March 1766. [SABR]

BELL, JAMES, Deacon of the Tailors of St Andrews, wife Christian Anderson, a bond, 1695. [NRS.B65.5.1.67]

BELL, JOHN, a glover in Cupar, a disposition, 1762. [NRS.B13.7.3/96]

BELL, ROBERT, a bailie of Burntisland, father of Jean Bell spouse of John Haxton the younger a skipper in Burntisland, a deed, 1735. [NRS.B9.11.13/79]

BELL, ROBERT, in St Andrews, was admitted as a burgess of St Andrews on 1 September 1773. [SABR]

BELL, THOMAS, a weaver, fourth son of Robert Bell the Deacon of the Weavers in St Andrews, was admitted as a burgess of St Andrews on 19 August 1763. [SABR]

BELL, WILLIAM, MA, minister at Auchtertool from 1636 until 1641. [F.V.78]

BELL, WILLIAM, master of the Marie of Pittenweem trading with Norway 1681-1683. [NRS.E72.9.10/14]

BENNET, HENRY, a maltman in Elie, and his wife Margaret Carstairs, a deed, 1657. [NRS.GD1.27.10]

BENNETT, HENRY, a ship carpenter from Elie, died aboard the Dolphin in North America, 1698, testament, 1707, Comm. Edinburgh. [NRS]

BENNET, LAWRENCE, in Poland, 1617, son of William Bennet of Balgonie. [NRS.RS31.1.30]

BENNET, WILLIAM, a merchant in Keidon, Lithuania, 1672, son of Reverend James Bennet in Auchtermuchty. [NRS.RD4.32.255]

BENNING, DAVID, a mariner from St Monance, died aboard the Smyrna Factor, probate 1696, Prerogative Court of Canterbury. [TNA]

BERRY, DAVID, master of the Providence of Kinghorn trading with Dunkirk in 1749. [NRS.E504.3.2]

BERTHLETT, WILLIAM, a weaver burgess of Cupar, husband of Elspeth Taylor, parents of William, James, and Elspeth, a bond of provision, 1722. [NRS.B13.7.2/20]

BETHLET, WILLIAM, a weaver and late Deacon of the Weavers of Cupar, a disposition, 1778. [NRS.B13.7.5/11]

BERVIE, DAVID, master of the Providence of Kinghorn trading with Riga in 1750. [NRS.E504.1.3]

BERWICK, DAVID, born 1754, a farmer in St Andrews, died 1826. [St Andrews gravestone]

BERWICK, JOHN, in Argyle, St Andrews, a bond, 1697. [NRS.B65.5.1/123]

BERWICK, JOHN, a meal-maker, son of James Bell a meal-maker burgess, was admitted as a burgess of St Andrews on 12 January 1771. [SABR]

BERWICK, WILLIAM, a ball-maker in St Andrews, a deed, 1685. [NRS.RD3.63.23]; a bond, 1707. [NRS.B65.5.2/42]

BETHUNE, ALEXANDER, born 1759, died 8 February 1838, husband of Alison Christie, born 1766, died 21 December 1840. [Abdie gravestone]

BETHUNE, GEORGE, a baker in Elie, and his wife Janet Corlett, a sasine, 1700. [NRS.GD1.27.20]

BETHUNE, HENRY, the younger of Blebo, was admitted as a burgess of St Andrews on 11 September 1761. [SABR]

BETHUNE, Sir HENRY LINDSAY, born 12 April 1787, a Major General, died in Persia on 19 February 1851. [Kilconquhar gravestone]

BETHUN, JOHN, master of the Helen of Crail trading with London in 1724. [NRS.CE52.1.3]

BETT, EDWARD, son of David Bett precentor of St Andrews, an indenture, 1695. [NRS.B65.5.1/104]

BEVERIDGE, HENRY, a skipper in Linktoun, master of the Pelican of Kirkcaldy trading with Ostend, Flanders, in 1673. [NRS.E72.9.8]

BEVERIDGE, HENRY, born 1798, son of Michael Beveridge in Kirkcaldy, died in Demerara in 1819. [BM.7.231]

BEVERIDGE, JAMES, a skipper in Burntisland, husband of Christian Ballantine, a deed, 1775. [NRS.B9.7.2/195]

BEVERIDGE, MALCOLM, was admitted as a burgess of St Andrews on 19 February 1760. [SABR]

BEVERIDGE, WILLIAM, a writer, testament, 1749. [NRS.SC20.27.1/4]

BIRRELL, ANDREW, a brewer and a bailie of Falkland, a deed, 1746. [NRS.CS228.B3.40]

BIRRELL, GEORGE, a Captain in the service of the Honorable East India Company in 1789, a sasine. [NRS.RS31.2124]

BIRRELL, JOHN, Deacon of the Butchers in Cupar, deeds, 1692, 1705. [NRS.RD4.71.968/1133; RD4.86.1307]

BIRRELL, PETER, a merchant in Cupar, husband of Grisel Gillan, a deed, 1697, testament, 1701. [NRS.RD4.80.912; CC20.2.8; 4.16]

BLACK, ALEXANDER, mate aboard the <u>Anna of Pittenweem</u> captured by the Turks near La Rochelle in France, then imprisoned at Sallee in 1678. [RPCS.6.288]

BLACK, ALEXANDER, a lawyer in Cupar, husband of Janet Manson, a disposition, 1765. [NRS.B13.7.3/168; 7.6/2]

BLACK, JAMES, master of the <u>Ann and Margaret of Leven</u> bound for Virginia in 1722. [NRS.E508.16.6]

BLACK, JOHN, alias Jan Swart, a merchant in Vlissingen, Zealand, heir to David Black uncle of Robert McNicol a smith in Dysart, a deed, 1791. [NRS.B21.5.3/271]

BLACK, PHILIP, a mariner and signaller aboard <u>HMS Greenwich</u>, son of Andrew Black a mariner in Anstruther, testament, 1719. Comm. Edinburgh. [NRS]

BLACK, ROBERT, a baker and a councillor of Burntisland in 1689. [RPCS.XIV.455]

BLACK, ROBERT, a weaver and a councillor of Burntisland in 1689. RPCS.XIV.455]

BLACK, WILLIAM, master of the <u>Grace of God of Anstruther</u> trading with Elsinore, Danzig and Norway in 1614. [RPCS.10.788]

BLACK, WILLIAM, son of James Black a weaver burgess of Dunfermline, was indentured under James Anderson a weaver burgess of Dunfermline for 4 years in 1796. [NRS.B20.6.12/405]

BLACK, WILLIAM, born 1794 in Fife, settled in Charleston, South Carolina, naturalised in Charleston in 1828. [NARA.M1183.1]

BLACKBURN, JOHN, a sailor in Kinghorn, testament, 1751, Comm. Edinburgh. [NRS]

BLACKWOOD, ADAM, a butcher and a councillor of Burntisland in 1689. [RPCS.XIV.455]

BLAIR, JOHN, MA, minister at Auchtertool from 1672 to 1682. [F.V.78]

BLAIR, WILLIAM, a burgess and guilds-brother of St Andrews, a bond, 1676. [NRS.RD4.40.125]

BLAIR, WILLIAM, was admitted as a burgess of St Andrews on 27 October 1756. [SABR]

BLAU, JOHN, a girdle-smith in Culross, a bond, 1714. [NRS.B12.5.1/15]

BLAU, MARGARET, in Culross, daughter of Alexander Blau, a tailor burgess of Culross, a will, 1749. [NRS.B12.5.2/139]

BLAW, THOMAS, son of James Blaw in Culross, married Margaret Morton daughter of John Morton in North Berwick, in the Scots Kirk in Rotterdam on 3 January 1714. [GAR]

BLOLOCH, JOSEPH, died 20 November 1789. [Beath gravestone]

BLYTH, JOHN, a shoemaker in Cupar, husband of Elizabeth Thomson, parents of Robert and David, a deed, 1776. [NRS.B13.7.4/329]

BLYTH, ROBERT, was admitted as a shoemaker burgess of Cupar on 29 September 1766. [CBR]

BOANS, WILLIAM, a meal-maker in St Andrews, a bond, 1694. [NRS.B65.5.1/62]

BOCCO, ANDREW, a saddler, died in 1777, husband of Jane Oliphant, born 1691, died 1775. [St Andrews gravestone]

BOGIE, JAMES, a burgess and guild-brother in Cupar, relict of Anna Turnbull, a deed, 1705. [NRS.RD2.90/2.523]

BOGLE, DAVID, was admitted as a burgess of Cupar on 29 September 1767. [CBR]

BOGLE, WILLIAM, a merchant in Kirkcaldy, aboard the Swan of Glasgow bound for Danzig in 1681. [NRS.E72.9.10]

BONAR, Master JOHN, was served heir to his father Master James Bonar of Greigston, on 21 April 1692. [NRS.Retours.Fife.1333]

BONTHRONE, ALEXANDER, born 1763, a brewer in Auchtermuchty, died 29 July 1829, husband of Agnes Lawson, born 1763, died 29 August 1833. [Auchtermuchty gravestone]

BONTHRON, ALEXANDER, in St Andrews, 1798. [NRS.E326.15.31]

BONTHRON, DAVID, master of the Exchange of Dysart trading with Konigsberg in 1750. [NRS.E504.1.3]

BONTHRON, DAVID, of Fafield, a Deed of Factory, 1754. [NRS.B65.5.4/53]

BONTHRON, JOHN, a lawyer in Cupar, a disposition, 1785. [NRS.B13.7.5/164]

BONTHRON, JOHN, born 1789 in Fife, emigrated to Philadelphia, Pennsylvania, in 1817, naturalised in Washington, DC, in 1828

BONTHRON, ROBERT, a sailor in Dubbyside, Markinch, testament, 1810, Comm. St Andrews. [NRS]

BONTHRON, THOMAS, a fisherman in Buckhaven, testament, 1808, Comm. St Andrews. [NRS]

BOOG, GEORGE, a skipper in Burntisland, spouse Ann Martin, a deed, 1732. [NRS.B9.11.13/13]

BORTHWICK, THOMAS, a mariner in Kilrenny, testament, 1637, Comm. St Andrews. [NRS]

BOSWELL, DAVID, of Craigincot, a charter, 1628. [NRS.GD26.3.717]

BOSWELL, JAMES, of Lochgelly, a charter, 1628. [NRS.GD26.3.717]

BOSWELL, JOHN, Commander of the frigate Batchelor a deed, 1672. [NRS.RD3.32.154]; skipper in Burntisland, testament, 1705, Comm. Edinburgh. [NRS]

BOSWELL, JOHN, Dean of Guild in Kirkcaldy, a petition, 1689. [RPCS.XIV.147]

BOUSE, HENRY, son of Thomas Bouse, schoolmaster of Wemyss, and later Newburgh, 1672-1673. [NRS.RD4.32.465; RD3.34.751.]

BOUSE, THOMAS, schoolmaster of Newburgh, 1680. [NRS.RD4.47.681]

BOUSIE, DAVID, a Deacon and a weaver burgess of Cupar, a deed, 1761. [NRS.B13.7.3/44]

BOUSIE, JOHN, a weaver in Cupar, spouse Janet Turnbull, a bond, 1679. [NRS.RD3.46.60]

BOWES, GEORGE, minister in Cupar, a bond of annuity, 1772. [NRS.B13.7.4/30]

BOWIE, ROBERT, a skipper in Dysart, testaments, 1751 and 1754, Comm. Edinburgh. [NRS]

BOWMAN, DAVID, from Kirkcaldy, a planter in Accomack County, Virginia, died 1785, probate 1786 Accomack.

BOWMAN, JANET, daughter of David Bowman a skipper in Kirkcaldy, testament, 1769, Comm. Edinburgh. [NRS]

BOWMAN, MARION, relict of Thomas Young a skipper in Kinghorn, testament, 1765, Comm. Edinburgh. [NRS]

33

BOWMAN, WILLIAM, a mariner in Kirkcaldy, husband of Janet Baxter, deeds, 1682-1686. [NRS.RD4.51.326; RD4.59.300]

BOWMAN, WILLIAM, a merchant in Dunnikier, a deed, 1763. [NRS.B21.5.1/273]

BOYACK, PATRICK, a tailor, eldest son of James Boyack a tailor in St Andrews, was admitted as a burgess of St Andrews on 5 June 1764. [SABR]

BOYD, JAMES, was admitted as a watch and clock-maker burgess of Cupar on 3 December 1795. [CBR]

BOYD, WILLIAM, a baker in Cupar, was admitted as a burgess of St Andrews on 6 March 1756. [SABR]

BOYTAR, ALEXANDER, master of the True Blue of Anstruther, trading with Tobago and Grenada from 1769 to 1771. [NRS.E504.22.15/16/17]

BOYTAR, ROBERT, master of the Charming Betty of Anstruther trading with Danzig in 1742. [NRS.E504.3.1]

BOYTER, THOMAS, born 1764, died 1838, husband of Isabel Arnot, born 1762, died 1806. [Balmerino gravestone]

BOYTAR, WILLIAM, a skipper in Cellardyke, husband of Janet Young, deeds, 1672-1687. [NRS.RD3.31.107; RD4.61.792]

BOYTAR, WILLIAM, master of the Charming Betty of Anstruther trading with Danzig in 1751. [NRS.E504.3.3]

BRABANDER, JOHN, a merchant in Cupar, was admitted as a burgess of St Andrews on 24 September 1765. [SABR]

BRABENDER, WILLIAM, a burgess of Newburgh by 1740. [NBR]

BRAID, DAVID, a tailor in St Andrews, a bond, 1695.
[NRS.B65.5.1/77]

BRAID, JOHN, second son of John Braid a merchant burgess of St
Andrews, was admitted as a burgess of St Andrews on 18 June
1771. [SABR]

BRAID, NORMAN, born 1791, son of John Braid and his wife
Catherine Porterfield, a surgeon, died in Borneo on 22 July 1811.
[St Andrews gravestone]

BRAID, WILLIAM, a burgess of St Andrews, a deed of factory,
1706. [NRS.B65.5.2/1]

BRAID, WILLIAM, a meal-maker, eldest son of Andrew Braid a
baker burgess of St Andrews was admitted as a burgess of St
Andrews on 29 December 1757. [SABR]

BRAID, WILLIAM, eldest son of John Braid a merchant burgess of
St Andrews, was admitted as a burgess of St Andrews on 18 June
1772. [SABR]

BRAND, ANDREW, schoolmaster of Dysart in 1666.
[NRS.RD2.18.227]

BRAND, JOHN, born 1703, a gardener in Valleyfield, died in
February 1783, husband of Elizabeth Masterton, born 1703, died
10 January 1778. [Culross Abbey gravestone]

BRAND, WILLIAM, a tailor and a councillor of Burntisland in 1689.
[RPCS.XIV.455]

BRIGGS, JOHN, of Kinnonmond, was served heir to his brother
David Briggs of Kinnonmond, on 21 August 1738. [NRS.S/H]

BRIGGS, JOHN, late of Calcutta, India, a sasine, 1790.
[NRS.RS31.2614]

BRIGGS, THOMAS, a mariner from Dysart, died aboard HMS London probate 1691, PCC. [TNA]

BRODIE, ALEXANDER, late of Madras, India, a sasine, 1789. [NRS.RS31.2121]

BROUGH, JAMES, master of the James and Margaret of Crail trading with Norway in 1669. [NRS.E72.7.3/4]

BROWN, ANDREW, a councillor of Burntisland in 1689. [RPCS.XIV.455]

BROWN, DAVID, born 1785, son of David Brown and his wife Helen Oswald, died 2 January 1830 in Jamaica. [Kingsbarns gravestone]

BROWN, EDWARD, master of the Cicilia of North Queensferry trading with Bilbao, Spain, in 1751. [NRS.E504.27.3]

BROWN, ELIZABETH, wife of Henry Rolland a meal-dealer in Culross, was served heir to her brother John Brown, son of Robert Brown of Barhill, on 19 March 1739. [NRS.S/H]

BROWN, GEORGE, a skipper in Boston, New England, was admitted as a burgess of St Andrews in 1741. [SABR]; from St Andrews, a member of the Scots Charitable Society of Boston in 1744. [NEHGS]

BROWN, JAMES, master of the Collin of North Queensferry bound for St Kitts in 1764. [NRS.E504.22.11]

BROWN, JOHN, shipmaster in Pittenweem, a warrant of the Privy Councill, 22 December 1691. [RPCS.XVI.665]

BROWN, JOHN, a wheelwright in St Andrews, 1696. [NRS.B65.5.1/75]

BROWN, JOHN, the town treasurer of Anstruther, was admitted as a burgess of St Andrews on 18 April 1758. [SABR]

BROWN, JOHN, son of Thomas Brown a tailor burgess, was admitted as a burgess of St Andrews on 21 April 1759. [SABR]

BROWN, JOHN, a burgess of Crail, was admitted as a burgess of St Andrews on 12 June 1772. [SABR]

BROWN, JOSEPH, a dyer in Kirkcaldy, was admitted as a burgess of St Andrews on 14 January 1766. [SABR]

BROWN, MARGARET, born 1736, died in June 1784. [Culross Abbey gravestone]

BROWN, PHILLIP, master of the Margaret of Elie trading with Gothenburg in 1742. [NRS.E504.27.1]

BROWN, ROBERT, a fisherman in Anstruther, testament, 1605, Comm. Edinburgh. [NRS]

BROWN, ROBERT, a cooper and mariner in West Wemyss, a deed, 1766. [NRS.B21.5.2/48]

BROWN, THOMAS, a merchant in Rotterdam, husband of Beiges Johnston, a sasine, 1608. [NRS.RS31.XI.208]

BROWN, THOMAS, master of the James of Kirkcaldy trading with Danzig in 1737. [NRS.CE52.1.4]

BROWN, THOMAS, Deacon of the Tailors of St Andrews, a contract, 1767. [NRS.B65.5.5/256]

BROWN, WALTER, master of the Diligence of Ely trading with Scandinavia and Hamburg in 1758-1759; master of the Expedition of Ely trading with Danzig in 1763. [NRS.E504.3.3]

BROWN, WILLIAM, schoolmaster of Culross, 1674-1682. [NRS.RD4.35.354; RD4.51.584]

BROWN, WILLIAM, from Wemyss, was admitted as a citizen of Rotterdam on 23 August 1719. [GAR]

BROWN, WILLIAM, Professor of Church History, died in 1791. [St Andrews gravestone]

BRUCE, ALEXANDER, born 1749 in Limekilns, died in St Andrews in 1822, husband of Agnes Marshall, born 1753, died 1815. [St Andrew's gravestone]

BRUCE, ANDREW. Professor of Divinity at St Mary's College, University of St Andrews, then minister of St Andrews from 1673 to 1679. [F.V.234]

BRUCE, ANDREW, master of the Betsy of Kinghorn, testament, 1761, Comm. Edinburgh. [NRS]

BRUCE, Lord EDWARD, died in Bergen op Zoom, Holland, in 1613. [Culross gravestone]

BRUCE, JOHN, the elder, Deacon of the Bakers of St Andrews, a deed, 1687. [NRS.RD2.67.432]

BRUCE, MORRICE, son of the late Arthur Bruce a burgess of St Andrews, was admitted as a burgess of St Andrews on 8 April 1758. [SABR]

BRUCE, ROBERT, born 1607 son of Sir John Bruce of Kincavil, minister at Aberdour from 1637 until his death in 1667, husband of Janet Watson, daughter of Captain Andrew Watson of Burntisland. [F.V.2]

BRUCE, ROBERT, of Grangemyre, was served heir to his father Robert Bruce a merchant bailie of Kinghorn on 3 July 1732. [NRS.S/H]

BRUCE, WILLIAM, a freeman wright in St Andrews, a contract of co-partnership, 1791. [NRS.B65.5.7/66]

BRUNTON, ISABEL, relict of John Ramsay a fisherman on the Isle of May, was admitted as a burgess of St Andrews on 25 December 1759. [SABR]

BRYDE, ALEXANDER, a maltman in St Andrews, a tack, 1710. [NRS.B65.5.2/116]

BRYDIE, ELIZABETH, wife of George Aiken in Leith, was served heir to her father Robert Brydie a burgess of Falkland on 18 December 1687. [NRS.Retours.Fife.1286]

BRYDIE, LILIAS, spouse of George Shaw a fisherman at Fife Ness, testament, 1746, Comm. St Andrews. [NRS]

BRYDIE, MARGARET, spouse of Andrew Corstorphine a skipper in Crail, testament, 1710, Comm. St Andrews. [NRS]

BRYSON, THOMAS, in Dempstertoun, Auchtermuchty, a deed, 1663. [NRS.GD63.140]

BUCHAN, JOHN, schoolmaster of Kirkcaldy Grammar School, husband of Euphan Morton, parents of John, 1672. [NRS.RD4.31.736]

BUCHAN, JOHN, second son Thomas Buchan a tailor burgess of St Andrews, was admitted as a burgess of St Andrews on 3 August 1759. [SABR]

BUCHANAN, ALLAN, born 1722, minister of Inverkeithing, died 8 March 1749. [Culross Abbey gravestone]

BUCHANAN, CHRISTIAN, widow of Thomas Borthwick a citizen of St Andrews, a bond, 1693. [NRS.B65.5.1/29]

BUCHANAN, ARCHIBALD, a butcher and a burgess of Culross, died 26 July 1717, husband of Janet Lambert, born 1660, died 4 September 1708. [Culross Abbey gravestone]

BUCHANAN, THOMAS, graduated MA from Glasgow University in 1684, minister at Dunfermline from 1710 until his death on 10 April 1715, husband of Grisell Glass. [F.V.30]

BUCHANAN, THOMAS, a tailor in St Andrews, was admitted as a burgess of St Andrews on 6 June 1764. [SABR]

BUDDO, JOHN, Deacon of the Weavers in St Andrews, 1728. [NRS.B65.5.3/61]

BUDDO, MARGARET, relict of Alexander Peattie a weaver in St Andrews, a dispensation, 1786. [NRS.B65.65.5.6/228]

BUDDO, THOMAS, born 1710, stamp-master and Convenor of the Seven Trades of St Andrews, died 6 June 1780. [St Andrews gravestone]

BUICK, Reverend JOHN, was admitted as a burgess of St Andrews on 16 July 1766. [SABR]

BUIST, GEORGE, born 1778 in Fife, educated at Edinburgh University, a minister who settled in Charleston, South Carolina, 1793, Principal of Charleston College in 1805, died in July 1852. [Old Scots gravestone, Charleston]

BULTIE, THOMAS, a citizen and merchant of St Andrews, a bond, 1676. [NRS.RD4.39.554]

BURN, GEORGE, a merchant in St Andrews, husband of Christian Dewie, a dispensation, 1764. [NRS.B65.5.5/130]

BURNS, JAMES, fourth son of John Burns a simple burgess, was admitted as a burgess of St Andrews on 11 March 1755. [SABR]

BURNS, JAMES and JOHN, merchants in St Andrews, a trust deed, 1795. [NRS.B65.5.8/13-20]

BURNS, JOHN, in Middle Mill, a bond, 1710. [NRS.B65.22.37]

BURNS, PATRICK, a merchant in Anstruther Easter, was admitted as a burgess of St Andrews on 11 December 1760. [SABR]

BURN, SAMUEL, a merchant in Kinghorn, was served heir to his uncle Samuel Simpson a merchant in Berwick, on 24 January 1753. [NRS.S/H]

BURNS, WILLIAM, was admitted as a sieve-wright burgess of Cupar on 5 October 1808. [CBR]

BURT, ANDREW, in Kinloch, Collessie, 1658. [RGS.X.671]

BURT, JAMES, born 1717, minister of Cairneyhill parish, died 12 August 1791, husband of Isabella Thomas, born 1739, died 13 July 1789. [Cairneyhill gravestone]

BUTTER, ROWLAND, was admitted as a burgess of St Andrews on 7 January 1758. [SABR]

BUTTERCASE, ANDREW, schoolmaster of Kemback, 1675. [NRS.GD7.SEC.2.56]

BUTTERS, JOHN H., born 2 April 1798, settled in New York on 28 August 1829, naturalised there on 26 September 1840.

BUTTON, PATRICK, in Newburgh, 1657. [RGS.X.622]

CALDER, JOHN, a merchant in St Andrews, husband of Agnes Hardie, bonds, 1683. [NRS.RD4.52.254; RD2.60.870]

CALLEND, Sir GEORGE, schoolmaster of Kilconquhar, testament, 1594, Commissariat of St Andrews. [NRS]

CALLENDAR, JOHN, born 1605, died 4 January 1664, husband of Margaret Hegein, born 1611, died 31 May 1662. [Culross West gravestone]

CAMPBELL, GEORGE, a student of divinity, was admitted as a burgess of St Andrews on 30 September 1765. [SABR]

CAMPBELL, JAMES, born 1729, a weaver, died 29 August 1795. [Culross Abbey gravestone]

CARMICHAEL, DAVID, of Balmedie, son of David Carmichael of Balmedie, was served heir to his mother Euphame Dempster on 5 May 1698. [NRS.Retours.Fife.1403]

CAMPBELL, WILLIAM, a student of divinity, was admitted as a burgess of St Andrews on 4 June 1761. [SABR]

CARFRAE, WILLIAM, was admitted as a burgess of St Andrews on 21 June 1762. [SABR]

CARMICHAEL, DAVID, tenant in Balgove, was admitted as a burgess of St Andrews on 7 June 1770. [SABR]

CARMICHAEL, DAVID BALFOUR, MD. was admitted as a burgess of St Andrews on 4 October 1771. [SABR]

CARMICHAEL, PATRICK, MA, minister of Aberdour from 1602-1610. [F.V.2]

CARMICHAEL, THOMAS, a maltman and citizen of St Andrews, a bond, 1692. [NRS.B65.5.1/7]

CARNES, JOHN, from Newburgh, died aboard HMS Mary, probate 1692, PCC. [TNA]

CARRY, JOHN, born 1749 in Fife, a stonemason, emigrated to Virginia in December 1773. [TNA.T47.9/11]

CARSAN, JOHN, minister at Abdie, a bond, 11 August 1691. [NRS.PC.12.16/103]

CARSTAIRS, ANDREW, son of George Carstairs, tenant in Kingsbarns, was admitted as a burgess of St Andrews on 28 March 1758. [SABR]

CARSTAIRS, BEATRIX, spouse of Angus Linklatter a skipper in Kirkcaldy, testament, 1704, Comm. St Andrews, [NRS]

CARSTAIRS, ELIZABETH, a widow in St Andrews, a bond, 1666. [NRS.RD4.17.237]

CARSTAIRS, JAMES, son of John Carstairs a writer and guilds-brother of St Andrews, was admitted as a burgess of St Andrews on 15 May 1762. [SABR]

CARSTAIRS, JOHN, of Kinneuchar, a Jacobite captured and imprisoned in Preston in 1715. [SAU.Cheap ms5.537]

CARSTAIRS, JOHN, son of David Carstairs a farmer in Boghall, a baker, was admitted as a burgess of St Andrews on 24 November 1772. [SABR]

CARSTAIRS THOMAS, in St Andrews, was admitted as a burgess of St Andrews on 26 December 1760. [SABR]

CARSTAIRS, THOMAS, born 1759 in Largo, an architect, settled in Pennsylvania in 1784. [SO]

CARSTAIRS. WILLIAM, eldest son of William Carstairs a guilds-brother of St Andrews, was admitted as a burgess of St Andrews on 19 February 1760. [SABR]

CARSWELL, PATRICK, schoolmaster of Auchtermuchty, 1622-1663, husband of Margaret Galbraith. [NRS.RS30.4.177; RD4.7.8]

CASSEL, JOHN, born 1779 in Cupar, educated at the University of St Andrews, a minister and a teacher, settled in Nova Scotia in 1811, died at Bocca Bec, St Patrick's, New Brunswick, on 18 July 1850. [SAU]

CATHCART, TAYLOR, son of James Cathcart of Pitcairly, educated at Glasgow University in 1793, settled in Jamaica. [MAGU.171]

CHAIPLAND, WILLIAM, a bailie of Burntisland in 1689.
[RPCS.XIV.455]

CHALMERS, ALEXANDER, s surgeon in Culross, was admitted as a
burgess and guilds-brother of Dunfermline on 3 May 1791. [DM]

CHALMERS, GEORGE, in Elie, was admitted as a burgess of St
Andrews on 2 July 1760. [SABR]

CHALMERS, JAMES, from Elie, a member of the Scots Charitable
Society of Boston, New England, in 1771. [NEHGS]

CHALMERS, JOHN, minister at Auchterderran from 1598 until
1638, died in 1642. [F.V.76]

CHALMERS, JOHN, jr, born 1605, MA St Andrews in 1627, minister
at Auchterderran from 1638 until his death on 14 November
1642, husband of {1] Isabel Scrymgeour, [2] Margaret Carmichael.
[F.V.76]

CHALMERS, JOHN, schoolmaster of Cupar, 1690. [SHS.4.2]

CHALMERS, JOHN, a merchant in Anstruther, was admitted as a
burgess of St Andrews on 4 October 1768. [SABR]

CHALMERS, THOMAS H., born 1793 in Fife, a grocer, was
naturalised in New York on 7 May 1821.

CHALMERS, WILLIAM, son of Dr John Chalmers minister of Elie,
was admitted as a burgess of St Andrews on 6 May 1760. [SABR]

CHALMERS, WILLIAM, born 1778, son of John Chalmers and his
wife Elizabeth Hall, died aboard the Queen at Rio de Janeiro,
Brazil, in 1800. [Anstruther Easter gravestone]

CHAPLAIN, ALEXANDER, master of the Ann and Isobel of
Burntisland trading with Lisbon in 1749. [NRS.E504.27.2]

CHAPLAIN, ANDREW, a mariner in Burntisland, a deed, 1690. [NRS.RD4.65.300]

CHEAP, JOHN, of Rossie, was admitted as a burgess of Cupar on 21 October 1795. [CBR]

CHEAPLAND, WILLIAM, in St Andrews, was served heir to his brother german David, son of William Cheapland a mariner in St Andrews on 19 January 1699. [NRS.Retours.Fife.1423]

CHIENE, JOHN, master of the Friendship of Crail in 1725. [NRS.CE52.1.3]

CHIENE, ROBERT, master of the Rising Sun of Anstruther whaling off Greenland, 1742-1762. [NRS.E504.3.1-4]

CHIESLIE, JOHN, minister of St Monance, was admitted as a burgess of St Andrews on 6 October 1765. [SABR]

CHISHOLM, JOHN, master of the Lady Janet of Pittenweem trading with Hampton, Virginia, in 1766; master of the Countess of Kelly of Pittenweem trading with New Providence in 1767, with Norfolk, Virginia, and with Hampton, Virginia, in 1768. [NRS.E504.3.3]

CHRISTIE, ALEXANDER, a mariner from Kinghorn, died aboard the Pineapple at Guinea, probate 1687, PCC. [TNA]

CHRISTIE, ANDREW, born 1788, son of Andrew Christie and his wife Margaret Dempster, died 26 November 1821 in India. [Cupar gravestone]

CHRYSTIE, DAVID, a bailie of Burntisland in 1689. [RPCS.XIV.455]

CHRISTIE, ROBERT, a merchant from Culross, husband of Margaret Sands, settled in Florida and Mexico in 1667. [RPCS.IV.297]

CHRISTIE, WILLIAM, schoolmaster of Auchtertool, a sasine, 1645. [NRS.RS30.15.123]

CLARK, GEORGE, eldest son of George Clark of Crowley and his wife Anna Hay, minister at Burntisland from 1672 until his death on 7 June 1688. [F.V.82]

CLARK, JOHN, in St Andrews, was admitted as a burgess of St Andrews on 27 December 1770. [SABR]

CLARK, WILLIAM, a bailie of Crail, was admitted as a burgess of St Andrews on 9 June 1759. [SABR]

CLEGHORN, JOHN, MA, minister at Burntisland from 1701 until 1711. [F.V.82]

CLELAND, ROBERT, a merchant in Crail, a Jacobite in 1745. [SHS.8.64/352]

CLEPHAN, ALEXANDER, a surgeon in Falkland, a bill of exchange, 1749. [NRS.GD1.392.167]

CLEPHANE, JAMES, born 20 October 1790, son of Thomas Clephane, emigrated from Kirkcaldy to Virginia in 1827, settled in Washington, D.C., naturalised there on 10 December 1833.

CLINTOUN, SAMUEL, schoolmaster of Dysart Grammar School, testament, 1713, Commissariat of St Andrews. [NRS]

COCHRANE, JOHN, educated at St Andrews University, a physician, emigrated to Kingston, Jamaica before 1744. [NRS.NRAS.726.5]

COCK, WALTER, schoolmaster of Auchtertool, 1690. [SHS.4.2]

COCKBURN, ISABELLA, born 1743, died 9 October 1811, wife of David Baird. [Beath gravestone]

COKKIE, or DONALDSON, JOHN, in Pittenweem, a deed, 1687. [NRS.GD62.228]

COLDSTREAM, ALEXANDER, a dyker in St Andrews, was admitted as a burgess of St Andrews on 22 December 1769. [SABR]

COLDSTREAM, ALEXANDER, born 1766, son of Alexander Coldstream and his wife Janet Goodfellow, died 6 August 1809 when bound for Domenica. [St Andrews gravestone]

COLDSTREAM, ALEXANDER, manager of Mitcham Estate in Dominica, eldest son of Alexander Coldstream in St Andrews, Fife, in 1799. [NRS.B65.5.8.104]

COLDSTREAM, JOHN, schoolmaster of Falkland, a deed, 1749. [NRS.GD1.392.166]

COLVILL, Lord ALEXANDER, of Culross, Rear Admiral of the White Squadron, testament, 1770, Comm. Edinburgh. [NRS]

COLLIER, JOHN, a limner, was admitted as a burgess of St Andrews on 26 March 1757. [SABR]

CONDIE, JOHN, heir of the late John Condie and Bessie Thomson in Kinloch, Collessie, 1658. [RGS.X.671]

CONGLETON, Captain CHARLES, of Craigtoun, was admitted as a burgess of St Andrews on 6 November 1765. [SABR]

COOKE, Major FRANCIS, born 1604, a soldier for 26 years, died 10 December 1646. [Aberdour gravestone]

COOK, JAMES, master of the George of Pittenweem trading with Iceland in 1689. [NRS.E72.9.27]

COOK, JAMES, master of the Mary of Pittenweem trading with Spain in 1731. [NRS.CE52.4.1]

COOK, JOHN, a skipper in Pittenweem, deeds, 1681/1683/1684. [NRS.RD3.51.126; RD3.55.131; RD3.69.159]

COOK, JOHN, the elder, a sailor from Kirkcaldy, died in the West Indies in 1699, testament, 1707, Comm. Edinburgh. [NRS]

COOK, ROBERT, a skipper in Pittenweem, 1635. [RPCS.6.572]

COOK, ROBERT, a mariner, was admitted as a burgess of Kirkcaldy in 1764. [KBR]

CORDIS, JOHN, master of the Evans of Burntisland bound for Antigua in 1775. [NRS.E504.20.8]

CORNFOOT, ANDREW, was served heir to his father Alexander Cornfoot of Balchrystie, on 19 April 1683. [NRS.Retours.Fife,1219]

CORSTORPHINE, ANDREW, a skipper burgess of Crail in 1692 [SBRS.XIII.128]; husband of Margaret Brydie, testament, 1710, Comm. St Andrews. [NRS]

CORSWELL, PATRICK, in Newburgh, 1657. [RGS.X.622]

COUPAR, ALEXANDER, schoolmaster of [1] Culross, 1656. [2] Edinburgh, [3] Leuchars, 1690; husband of Mary Christie. [NRS.RD4.11.942; RD4.17.101; RD4.18.329; RD4.38.168, RD4.41.741, RD3.46.265; RD4.372; RS30.20.339][SHS.4.2]

COUPAR, ALEXANDER, eldest son of Alexander Coupar a meal-maker burgess of St Andrews, was admitted as a burgess of St Andrews on 9 September 1773. [SABR]

COUPAR, DAVID, son of the late Alexander Coupar a mariner in St Andrews, was admitted as a burgess of St Andrews on 19 July 1757. [SABR]

COUPAR, JAMES, second son of Alexander Coupar a burgess of St Andrews, was admitted as a burgess of St Andrews on 12 August 1774. [SABR]

COUPAR, JOHN, eldest son of Alexander Coupar a wright, was admitted as a burgess of St Andrews on 10 September 1756. [SABR]

COUPAR, JOHN, at Argyll Bridge, St Andrews, was admitted as a burgess of St Andrews on 7 January 1758. [SABR]

COUPAR, SIMON, graduated MA from Edinburgh University in 1667, minister at Dunfermline from 1686 to 1693, died in Edinburgh on 20 September 1710, husband of Elizabeth Meldrum. [F.V.29]

COUPAR, THOMAS, in St Andrews, was admitted as a burgess of St Andrews on 6 January 1758. [SABR]

COWTRIE, JAMES, a skipper in Elie, master of the Margaret of Elie, a charter party, 1664. [NRS.RD4.11.780]

COWTRIE, JAMES, a skipper in Earlsferry, 1684. [NRS.RD4.54.251]

COULTRIE, JAMES, a fisherman in Largo, 1706. [NRS.GD26.15.21]

CRAIG, ANN, born 1756, a servant from Anstruther, emigrated via Leith aboard the Friendship bound for Philadelphia, Pennsylvania, on 9 May 1775. [TNA.T47.12]

CRAIG, JAMES, schoolmaster of Elie, husband of Janet Robertson, a sasine, 1623. [NRS.RS30.5.6]

CRAIG, JAMES, schoolmaster of Dysart, sasine, 1643. [NRS.RS30.15.12]

CRAIG, JAMES, eldest son of John Craig a guilds-brother of St Andrews, was admitted as a burgess of St Andrews on 20 September 1758. [SABR]

CRAIG, JOHN, a skipper from Kinghorn, an assessor of the Scots Court at Veere, Zealand, 1719. [NRS.RH11.2]

CRAIG, JOHN, master of the Fisher of Dysart trading with Rotterdam in 1730. [NRS.CE52.4.1]

CRAMBIE, PATRICK, was served heir to his father Patrick Crambie a merchant burgess of Cupar, on 28 August 1688. [NRS.Retours.Fife.1297]

CRAMMOND, PATRICK, was admitted as a burgess of Crail in 1760. [CBR]

CRAWFORD, ELIZABETH, a merchant in Anstruther West, a Jacobite in 1745. [SHS.8.64/352]

CRAWFORD, JAMES, of Mountwhanie, a tacksman of the Inland Excise of Fife, 1689. [RPCS.XIV.73]

CRAWFORD, JOHN, son of Thomas Crawford in Kirkcaldy, a sailor aboard the Rising Sun bound for Darien in 1699, testament, 1707, Comm. Edinburgh. [NRS]

CRAWFORD, WILLIAM, a skipper in Crail, 1692. [SBRS.13.128]

CRAWFORD, WILLIAM, born 1794, son of William Crawford, a Lieutenant of the 16th Bengal Native Infantry, died in Calcutta on 6 April 1818. [St Andrews gravestone]

CRIE, JOHN, a burgess of Newburgh by 1740. [NBR]

CROLL, JOHN, a burgess of Newburgh by 1740. [NBR]

CUMING, THOMAS, a sailor from Culross, aboard the Endeavour bound for Darien in 1698, testament, 1707, Comm. Edinburgh. [NRS]

CUMINS, ANDREW, master of the John and Sarah of Limekilns trading with Rotterdam in 1730. [NRS.CE52.4.1]

CUMMINS, THOMAS, from Wemyss, married Margaret Gray, in the Scots Kirk in Rotterdam on 1 December 1700. [GAR]

CUNNINGHAM, ALEXANDER, a sailor from Dysart, aboard the Unicorn bound for Darien in 1698, testament, 1707, Comm. Edinburgh. [NRS]

CUNNINGHAM, ALEXANDER, an Admiral of the Royal Navy, died in Anstruther on 10 March 1799. [SM.61.210]

CUNNINGHAM, JAMES, born 1722, a soldier of the Scots Brigade in the Netherlands, died in 1793 in Brompton. [Inverkeithing gravestone]

CUNNINGHAM, JOHN, born 1575, a mariner from Crail, master of the Danish vessel the Lion bound from Copenhagen, Denmark to Greenland in 1605, later from Denmark to Labrador and Greenland in 1606, in 1619 he was appointed Governor of Vardohuus in northern Norway, died in 1651. [DCB.I.243]

CUNNINGHAM, THOMAS, from Crail, a grocer in Stockholm, Sweden, drowned in 1697, buried in Riddarsholms Church. [SHR.XXV.292]

CURRIE, JAMES, master of the Nancy of Anstruther trading with Riga, in 1757. [NRS.E504.3.2]

CUSHELL, MICHAEL, valet to the Earl of Kelly, was admitted as a burgess of St Andrews on 5 October 1756. [SABR]

CUTHBERT, DAVID, born 1715, died 1781, father of James Cuthbert of Berthier, His Majesty's Legislative Councillor in Canada. [Culross gravestone]

CUTHBERT, JAMES, a blacksmith, eldest son of James Cuthbert a blacksmith in St Andrews, was admitted as a burgess of St Andrews on 9 September 1757. [SABR]

DAIRSIE, WILLIAM, a skipper burgess of Anstruther Wester, 1635/ [RPCS.6.572]

DALGLEISH, DAVID, a shipmaster in St Andrews, 1650. [SAU.ms36220/601]

DALGLEISH, JAMES, schoolmaster of Dunfermline Grammar sasine, 1633. [NRS.RS30.10.475]

DALGLEISH, JOHN, a shipmaster in St Andrews, husband of Catherine Anderson, parents of David Dalgleish, testament, 1617, Comm. St Andrews. [NRS]

DALL, WILLIAM, born 1797, died in Racine, Wisconsin, on 24 May 1877. [Newburgh gravestone]

DALRYMPLE, DAVID, from St Kitts, in Methil in 1766. [NRS.SC20.36.12]

DALRYMPLE, JAMES, schoolmaster of Auchtermuchty, 1690. [SHS.4.2]

DALRYMPLE, JOHN HAMILTON, born 1777, Customs Collector at Montego Bay, Jamaica, died 7 August 1804. [St Andrews gravestone]

DALRYMPLE, ROBERT, from Burntisland, a member of the Scots Charitable Society of Boston in 1739. [NEHGS]

DAMANCELL, CHARLES, in Strathmiglo, was granted the lands, lordship and barony of Newbotle near Edinburgh, by Oliver Cromwell on 2 July 1658. [RGS.X.659]

DASSON, WILLIAM, a maltman and burgess of Culross, died 17 April 1663. [Culross West gravestone]

DAVIDSON, ALEXANDER, born 1788, son of John Davidson, a mariner who died in Bengal, India, on 23 October 1809. [Kilrenny gravestone]

DAVIDSON, GEORGE, from Kirkcaldy, a burgess of Bergen in Norway, 1631. [SAB]

DAVIDSON, Captain GEORGE, born 1774, son of John Davidson, died at Isle de France on 22 February 1810. [Kilrenny gravestone]

DAVIDSON, HENDRIE, in Blacklaw, was jointly granted the lands and barony of Cardoun in the parish of Auchterderran in November 1657. [RGS.X.627]

DAVIDSON, PETER, a thief in Strathmiglo, was transported to the colonies in 1769. [SM.31.73]

DAVIDSON, ROBERT, from Cupar, a soldier, married Adriaen Michaels in Breda, the Netherlands, in 1594. [Breda Marriage Register]

DAVIDSON, WILLIAM, a sailor in St Andrews, testament, 1629, Comm. St Andrews. [NRS]

DAVIE, JOHN, was served heir to his brother german George Davie, a sailor in Northferry, son of Walter Davie a sailor there, on 18 October 1695. [NRS.Retours.Fife.1377]

DAW, ANDREW, master of the Nicolas of Crail trading with Stockholm, Sweden, in 1681. [NRS.E72.7.7]

DAW, JOHN, master of the privateer Consort of Crail in 1627. [RPCS.2.26]

DAWSON, DAVID, a mariner and burgess of Pittenweem, August 1623. [RPCS.13.352]

DAWSON, JAMES, a bailie of Burntisland in 1689. RPCS.XIV.455]

DEAS, DAVID, in Castletoun of Arngask, a charter, 1744. [NRS.GD1.13.10]

DEMPSTER, JAMES, born 1667, died 15 March 1745, husband of Agnes Wisheart, born 1682, died 1746. [Auchtermuchty gravestone]

DEMPSTER, JAMES, born 1760 in Cupar, died 18 October 1802 in Georgia. [Georgia gravestone]

DEMPSTERTOUN, PATRICK, a mariner burgess of Pittenweem, testament, 1620, Comm. St Andrews. [NRS]

DEWAR, AGNES, was served co-heir to her father Andrew Dewar a mariner burgess of Burntisland on 3 May 1692. [NRS.Retours.Fife.1334]

DEWAR, JANET, was served co-heir to her father Andrew Dewar a mariner burgess of Burntisland on 3 May 1692. [NRS.Retours.Fife.1334]

DEWAR, JOHN, a bailie of Burntisland in 1689. RPCS.XIV.455]

DEWAR, JOHN, schoolmaster of Scoonie, 1690. [SHS.4.2]

DEWAR, JOHN, from St Andrews, a Jacobite in 1745, killed at Culloden in 1746. [SHS.8.64]

DEWAR, WILLIAM, born 1744, a blacksmith from Burntisland, bound for Antigua in 1774. [TNA.T47.12]

DICK, JOHN, a mariner in St Andrews, lease of a ship, 1670. [NRS.RD2.28.207]

DICKENSON, JOHN, from St Andrews, a chaplain aboard HMS Mary, probate, 1700, Prerogative Court of Canterbury. [TNA]

DINNES, JOHN, a mariner aboard the Anna of Pittenweem captured near La Rochelle in France, and imprisoned at Sallee, North Africa, by the Turks in 1678. [Edinburgh Burgh Records, a petition in 1679]

DISHER, AGNES, born 1784, wife of George Mackay, died 6 October 1817. [Crombie gravestone]

DISHINGTON, GEORGE, a skipper in St Monance, husband of Anna Binning, testament, 1688, Comm. St Andrews. [NRS]

DISHINGTON, THOMAS, master of the John of Anstruther trading with Norway in 1670. [NRS.E72.9.4]

DONALD, JAMES, born in February 1747, son of David Donald a cordiner and his wife Elizabeth Duncan, died on 24 October 1747. [Culross Abbey gravestone]

DONALDSON, JAMES, a mill-wright at Grange of Lindores, a bond, 1800. [NRS.CS271.441]

DONALDSON, JOHN, a shoemaker and a councillor of Burntisland in 1689. RPCS.XIV.455]

DONALDSON, THOMAS, a mariner in Pittenweem, testament, 1699, Comm. St Andrews. [NRS]

DOUGALL, JOHN, master of the Janet of Kirkcaldy trading between Kirkcaldy and Holland in 1681-1682. [NRS.E72.9.10/13]

DOUGLAS, ALEXANDER, from Culross, was admitted as a citizen of Rotterdam in 1719. [GAR]

DOUGLAS, JAMES, the elder, a councillor of Burntisland in 1689. RPCS.XIV.455]

DOUGLAS, JOHN, master of the Sally of Kirkcaldy at Kingston, Jamaica, in March 1796. [NRS.AC7.72]

DOUGLAS, JOHN, born 1784 in Dunfermline, a brewer, distiller and storekeeper, settled in Whitestown, Oneida County, New York, naturalised in New York on 2 May 1821 and on 11 October 1830.

DOUGLAS, ROBERT, in Jamaica and in Burntisland, testament 20 August 1816 Comm. St Andrews. [NRS]

DOUGLAS, WILLIAM, a wright in Kinghorn, 1800. [NRS.CS271.70447]

DRONE, GEORGE, born 1676, a merchant in Abernethie, died 11 November 1756, husband of Jean Rutherford, died 15 May 1743, parents of Patrick Drone, died 11 November 1756. [Auchtermuchtie gravestone]

DRON, JOHN, a burgess of Newburgh by 1740. [NBR]

DRUMMOND, GEORGE, a tinker in Pathhead, a horse-thief, was transported to the colonies in April 1773. [AJ.1321]

DRUMMOND, KATHERINE, daughter of James Drummond in Kelty, died in Kingston, Jamaica, in 1806. [SM.69.77]

DRUMMOND, ROBERT, a skipper in Anstruther Wester in 1635. [RPCS.6.572]

DRUMMOND, THOMAS, born 1742, son of James Drummond of Lundin and his wife Rachel Bruce, settled in New York by 1768, a Loyalist, died in Bermuda in 1780. [SP.V.]

DRYSDALE, DAVID, a sailor from Culross, husband of Jean Archibald, bound for Darien aboard the Rising Sun in 1699, testament, 1707, Comm. Edinburgh. [NRS]

DRYSDALE, ISOBELL, vintner in Culross, widow of Robert Spittle a shoemaker in Culross, a deed, 1776. [NRS.B12.5.3/326-329]

DRYSDALE, JAMES, born April 1752, son of James Drysdale and his wife Christen Anderson, died 23 March 1753. [Culross Abbey gravestone]

DUDDINGSTONE, JAMES, a skipper in Crail in 1635. [RPCS.6.572]

DUDDINGSTONE, WILLIAM, son of William Duddingstone late bailie of Crail, and Margaret Miller, daughter of Andrew Miller a baker in Crail, a marriage contract, 1707. [NRS.GD1.27.22]

DUNBAR, ALEXANDER, son of the sheriff of Moray, graduated MA from King's College, Aberdeen, in 1658, minister at Dunfermline from 1676 until 1676, died on 22 March 1678. [F.V.29]

DUNCAN, ALEXANDER, from Dysart, was admitted as a citizen of Rotterdam in 1740. [GAR]

DUNCAN, ANDREW, master of the Concord of St Andrews, a brigantine, trading with Gothenburg, Sweden, in 1751. [NRS.E504.27.2]

DUNCAN, ARCHIBALD, a mariner in Kinghorn, testament, 1809, Comm. St Andrews. [NRS]

DUNCAN, JAMES, from Crail, married Margaret Carlyle from Cramond, in the Scots Kirk in Rotterdam on 11 April 1708. [GAR]

DUNCAN, JAMES, born 1772, son of William Duncan, a wright in Gauldry, and his wife Agnes Sime, died in Savannah, America, in 1798. [Kilmany gravestone]

DUNCAN, JOHN, born 1775, a shoemaker in Gauldry, died 5 July 1840, husband of Elizabeth Paton, born 1782, died 14 July 1838. [Balmerino gravestone]

DUNDAS, DAVID, from St Andrews, was admitted as a citizen of Cracow, Poland, in 1576. [Lib.Jur.Civ. Cracow, 1555-1601, fo.55]

DUNKIE, ALEXANDER, from Dysart, was admitted as a citizen of Rotterdam on 11 November 1740. [RA]

DURHAM, Admiral Sir PHILIP HENDERSON CALDERWOOD, of Largo, born 29 July 1763 in Largo, died in Naples, Italy, on 2 April 1845. [Largo gravestone]

DURIE, GEORGE, probably from Thornton, a seaman aboard HMS Sutherland, died in 1758 possibly at the Siege of Louisbourg, probate 1758, Halifax County, Nova Scotia.

DURIE, HENRY, a mariner burgess of Kirkcaldy, husband of Isobel Boswell, 1636. [RGS.IX.539]

DURKIE, ALEXANDER, from Dysart, and Katherine Palmer from Edinburgh, were married in the Scots Kirk in Rotterdam on 26 September 1767. [GAR]

ECKFORD, JOHN, son of John Eckford and his wife Janet Buntine, Captain of the Honorable East Company ship Lady Dundas, died in 1829. [Dunfermline gravestone]

EDMUNDSTOUNE, JAMES, of Carden, a bond, 1683. [NRS.GD1.49.34]

ELLIOT, ANDREW, born 1674, minister at Auchtertool from 1700 until his death on 1 July 1745. [F.V.78]

ERSKINE, CHARLES, master of the Defiance of Anstruther trading with Danzig in 1750. [NRS.E504.3.3]

ERSKINE, DAVID, master of the St Andrew of Crail trading with Memel in 1770. [NRS.E504.3.4]

ERSKINE, GEORGE, a skipper in Crail, testament, 1759, Comm. Edinburgh. [NRS]; master of the Bonny Jean of Pittenweem trading with Gothenburg and Hamburg in 1756-1757. [NRS.E504.3.3]

ERSKINE, Sir JOHN, of Cambo, was served heir to his brother Sir Charles Erskine of Cambo who died in February 1753, on 25 December 1753. [NRS.S/H]

ERSKINE, RALPH, born 15 March 1685 in Northumberland, son of Henry Erskine and his wife Margaret Halcro, educated at Edinburgh University, minister at Dunfermline from 1716 until 1740, died 6 November 1752. Husband of [1] Margaret Dewar, [2] Margaret Simson. [F.V.30]

ERSKINE, ROBERT, born 7 September 1735 in Dunfermline, son of Reverend Ralph Erskine and his wife Margaret Simson, Geographer and Surveyor General of the US Army, died in America on 2 October 1780. [F.5.30]

FAICHNEY, DAVID, a burgess of Newburgh by 1740. [NBR]

FAIR, JOHN, son of John Fair and his wife Helen, paymaster of the 63rd Regiment of Foot, died in Barbados on 4 July 1808. [Kilconquhar gravestone]

FAIR, THOMAS, son of John Fair and his wife Helen, a Captain in the service of the Honorable East India Company, died in Goa on 24 December 1822. [Kilconquhar gravestone]

FAIRFOULL, DAVID, a notary in Newburgh, husband of Eupham Leslie, a sasine, 1621. [NRS.RS31.III.245]

FAIRFOULL, JAMES, schoolmaster of Ceres, 1690. [SHS.4.2]

FAIRFOULL, JAMES, master of the Euphame of Pittenweem trading with Danzig in 1752, [NRS.E504.3.3]; master of the Jolly Bachelor of St Andrews trading with Gothenburg, Sweden, in 1755. [NRS.E504.3.3]

FAIRFOULL, JOHN, son of John Fairfoull a meal-maker in St Andrews, tacks, 1707, 1709, was admitted as a burgess of St Andrews on 10 July 1714. [NRS.B65.5.2/37/69][SABR]

FAIRFOULL, ROBERT, a mariner in St Andrews in 1735.
[NRS.B65.22.34]

FAIRFOULL, THOMAS, born 1747, died 25 July 1823, husband of
Ann Landel, born 1760, died 27 November 1827. [St Andrews
gravestone]

FAIRFOULL, WILLIAM, eldest son of John Fairfoull in St Andrews,
was admitted as a burgess of St Andrews on 3 January 1712.
[SABR]

FALCONER, ALEXANDER, from St Andrews, died in Franklin
County, North Carolina, on 17 March 1818. [Raleigh Register:
3.1818]

FARMER, DAVID, schoolmaster of Strathmiglo, husband of Isobel
Miller, 1661. [NRS.RS30.18.271; RD3.1.19]

FARMER, JOHN, Baron Clerk of Anstruther, and his wife Anna
Morton, 1689. [RPCS.XIV.515]

FERGUSON, ALEXANDER, a skipper in Peterhead, was admitted as
a burgess of St Andrews on 4 June 1765. [SABR]

FERGUSON, JAMES, a mariner from Fife, husband of Anna
Abercromby, aboard the Caledonia bound for Darien in 1698,
testament, 1707, Comm. Edinburgh. [NRS]

FERGUSON, ROBERT, born 1685, a maltman, died in November
1739. [Culross Abbey gravestone]

FERNIE, ALLAN, was admitted as a merchant burgess and guilds-
brother of Cupar on 2 March 1786. [CBR]

FERNIE, JAMES, a maltman in St Andrews, deceased, relict
Christian Band, a tack, 1710. [NRS.B65.5.2/124]

FERNIE, JAMES, son of John Fernie, a maltman in St Andrews,
testament, 1732, Comm. St Andrews. [NRS]

FERNIE, JOHN, in St Andrews, a deed in 1707. [NRS.RD3.114.121]

FERRIER, GEORGE, born 1771, died 2 March 1814, husband of Elizabeth Bayne, born 1767, died 6 February 1840, parents of James Ferrier in Montreal. [Auchtermuchty gravestone]

FERRY, DAVID, born 1664, schoolmaster, died 1 June 1726. [Auchtermuchty gravestone]

FINLAY, ANDREW, and JAMES, wrights in St Andrews, a deed, 1770. [NRS.B65.22.36]

FINDLAY, JAMES, Portioner of Balchrystie, and his wife Margaret Mackie, brewers in Newburn, a petition, 1689. [RPCS.XIV.73]

FINDLAY, JOHN, son of Mathew Findlay a butcher in Gallatown, was indentured to George Rutherford a skipper in Dysart for 3.5 years from 11 February 1786. [NRS.B21.5.3/190]

FINDLAY, THOMAS, of Balkirsty, son of James Findlay, settled in Barbados before 1741, father of Thomas, Isabella, Margaret, and Helen, died in June 1760. [NRS.RD3.224.9; S/H.31.10.1765]

FINLAY, WILLIAM, from Fife, a member of the Scots Charitable Society of Boston, New England, in 1739. [NEHGS]

FINLAYSON, JAMES, born 1741, died 4 June 1782, husband of Catherine Normand, born 1753, died 28 June 1834. [Balmerino gravestone]

FINLAYSON, JANET, born 1714, wife of Donald Meiklejohn, died 17 May 1770. [Culross Abbey gravestone]

FLEMING, ALEXANDER, a sailor from Dysart, aboard the St Andrew bound for Darien in 1698, testament, 1707, Comm. Edinburgh. [NRS]

FLEMING, GEORGE, in Balbuthie, a Crown Charter, 6 December 1653. [RGS.X.206]; a petition, 12 September 1689. [RPCS.XIV.264]

FLEMING, JOHN, from Dysart, married Elizabeth Warren from Linlithgow, in the Scots Kirk in Rotterdam on 21 February 1733. [GAR]

FLEMING, JOHN, a mariner in Rotterdam, eldest son of Andrew Fleming a burgess of Dysart, a dispensation in favour of John Christie a mariner in Dysart, 10 February 1773. [NRS.B21.5,2/205]

FLETCHER, DAVID, in St Andrews, in October 1798. [NRS.E326.15.31]

FLUCKER, JAMES, from Kirkcaldy, a seaman aboard the Veere on 1 May 1646. [ZA]

FOGGO, JOHN, a writer in St Andrews, a deed, 1714. [NRS.RD2.103.2.678]

FOGGO, JOHN, a teacher, was admitted as a burgess and guilds-brother of Dunfermline on 26 April 1798. [DM]

FOORD, WILLIAM, a sailor from Burntisland, husband of Euphan Robertson, bound for Darien aboard the Caledonia in 1698, testament, 1707, Comm. Edinburgh. [NRS]

FORBES, ALEXANDER, born 1726, from Wemyss, a Jacobite in 1745, captured and transported to Jamaica in 1747. [SHS.2.200] [TNA.CO137.58]

FORBES, DUNCAN, the younger, of Birdsyards, was admitted as a burgess of St Andrews on 19 August 1727. [SABR]

FORBES, DUNCAN, from Kirkcaldy, a Jacobite in 1745. [SHS.8.260]

FORBES, JAMES, portioner of Kilmany, a deed, 1631. [NRS.GD7.sec.1/38]

FORBES, JOHN, of Culloden, was admitted as a burgess of St Andrews on 19 August 1727. [SABR]

FORBES, JOHN, born 1707 at Pittencreiff, Dunfermline, a Brigadier General during the French and Indian Wars, died in Philadelphia on 11 March 1759. [Christ Church gravestone, Philadelphia, Pennsylvania]

FORBES, JOHN, in St Andrews in October 1798. [NRS.E326.15.31]

FOREST, THOMAS, lately from the East Indies, purchaser of the estate of Cluny, versus Isobel Ross, daughter of Thomas Ross of Calrossie, Declarator of Marriage, 1769. [NRS.CC8.6.467]

FORMAN, JAMES, a miller and land labourer in St Andrews, testament, 1765, Comm. St Andrews. [NRS]

FORRESTER, ANDREW, minister at Dunfermline from 1610 to 1616. [F.V.27]

FORRESTER, JAMES, a councillor of Burntisland in 1689. [RPCS.XIV.455]

FORRESDALE, CHRISTIAN, relict of John Oliphant a mariner in Kirkcaldy, testament, 1780, Comm. St Andrews. [NRS]

FORSYTH, WALTER, a butcher in Falkland, a deed, 1799. [NRS.CS226.B11.33]

FORTUNE, GEORGE, master of the Euphame of Pittenweem, trading with Danzig in 1747 and 1750, [NRS.E504.3.2]; master of the Alliance of Pittenweem from Bo'ness to the Chesapeake in 1753. [NRS.CE57-58]

FOSTER, ANDREW, born 25 June 1772, son of John Foster and his wife Barbara Fairnie, a merchant in New York by 1798, married

[1] Ann Giraud, [2] Ann Ten Eyck, father of Jacob Foster, died on 25 December 1849 in New York, [ANY.I.334]

FOTHERINGHAM, ANDREW, a weaver, son-in-law of John Wright a weaver burgess, was admitted as a burgess of Dunfermline on 24 November1785, [DM]

FOTHERINGHAM, GEORGE, a burgess of Newburgh by 1740. [NBR]

FOTHERINGHAM, NORMAN, from Culross, married Janet Kelck from Rotterdam, in the Scots Kirk in Rotterdam on 5 May 1717. [GAR]

FOULIS, WILLIAM, born 1716, a wright in St Andrews, died on 12 April 1774, husband of Janet Reid, born 1731, died 25 May 1815, parents of William Foulis a smith. [St Andrews gravestone]

FRASER, ALEXANDER, a merchant in St Andrews, deeds, 1769-1771. [NRS.B65.5.5/295; B65.22.36]

FRASER, ALEXANDER, in St Andrews, in October 1798. [NRS.E326.15.31]

FRASER, ANNE, from Freuchie, settled in Northampton County, Virginia, by 1776, spouse of Kendall Harmonson. [NRS.RD2.220.1267]

FRASER, DAVID, a merchant in St Andrews, testament, 1727, Comm. St Andrews. [NRS]

FRASER, DAVID, a writer in St Andrews, heir to his father Alexander Fraser a merchant there in 1756; a deed in 1769. [NRS.S/H; B65.5.5/277; B65.22.37]

FRASER, DAVID, from Parbroath, a member of the Scots Charitable Society of Boston, New England, in 1743. [NEHGS]

FRASER, JOHN, a merchant in St Andrews, testament, 1732, Comm. St Andrews. [NRS]

FYFFE, JAMES, a traveller in Tarnova, Poland, son of Gilbert Fyffe in Forgan and his wife .... Gray, a birth brief granted on 5 April 1610 by Dundee Town Council. [DCA]

FYFFE, THOMAS, a mariner in St Andrews, husband of Agnes Livingstone, a testament, 1638, Comm. St Andrews. [NRS]

GAIRDNER, WILLIAM, a sailor from Abbotshall, husband of Agnes Davidson, bound aboard the Unicorn to Darien in 1698, testament, 1707, Comm. Edinburgh. [NRS]

GARDIE, HENRY, portioner of Newburgh, a tack, 1750. [NRS.GD214.328]

GARDNER, THOMAS, born 1716 in Birkhill, died there on 23 October 1806. [Balmerino gravestone]

GAY, JOHN, from Dysart, a gunner aboard the Lion of Zeeland in 1631. [ZA]

GEDD, ALEXANDER, a councillor of Burntisland in 1689. [RPCS.XIV.455]

GED, ROBERT, master of the Happy Janet of Burntisland trading with Rotterdam in 1754. [NRS.E504.27.3]

GEDDIE, ELIZABETH, was served heir portioner to her father John Geddie of St Nicholas, on 10 March 1691. [NRS.Retours.Fife.1452]

GEDDIE, HELEN, wife of James Lentrone of St Foord, was served heir portioner to her father John Geddie of St Nicholas, on 10 March 1691. [NRS.Retours.Fife.1452]

GEDDIE, JOHN, from Kinkell, a soldier in Holland, 1640. [NRS.S/H.1640]

GEDDIE, MICHAEL, a skipper in St Andrews, testament, 1706, Comm. St Andrews. [NRS]

GIBSON, JOHN, a skipper in St Andrews, testament, 1711, Comm. St Andrews. [NRS]

GIBSON, WALTER, master of the Mary of Inverkeithing was captured by Turkish pirates when sailing from Scotland to Lisbon via Nantes, and imprisoned at Salee in November 1674. [RPCS.IV.294]

GIBSON, WALTER, only son of the late John Gibson a guilds-brother of St Andrews, was admitted as a burgess of St Andrews, on 29 December 1757. [SABR]

GIBSON, WILLIAM, from Kirkcaldy, a gunner aboard the Arms of Zeeland in 1644. [ZA]

GILBERT, JOHN, a burgess of Newburgh by 1740. [NBR]

GILBERT, WILLIAM, a mariner in Kilrenny, husband of Beatrix Slekirk, a sasine, 1656. [NRS.RS30.20.495]

GILCHRIST, HENRY, a seaman from Burntisland, aboard the Caledonia bound for Darien in 1698, testament, 1707, Comm. Edinburgh. [NRS]

GILCHRIST, JOHN, a carpenter journeyman from Dysart, aboard the Benjamin of the Bay of Honduras, 1785. [NRS.AC9.3244]

GILLESPIE, ANDREW, a mariner in Crail, who was lost on a voyage to the West Indies, testament, 27 August 1811, Comm. St Andrews. [NRS]

GILLESPIE, ALEXANDER, master of the James of Elie trading with Rotterdam in 1683. [NRS.E72.9.17]

GILLESPIE, JAMES, a clerk in Inverkeithing, son in law of John Cusine a merchant in Dunfermline, was admitted as a burgess of Dunfermline on 13 January 1795. [DM]

GLASS, CUDBERT THORNHILL, born 1793, eldest son of Lieutenant Colonel Glass in St Andrews, died 14 December 1830. [South Park gravestone, Calcutta]

GLASS, PATRICK, a burgess of Newburgh by 1742. [NBR]

GLAS, WILLIAM, son of Reverend Patrick Glas in Crail, was admitted as a burgess of St Andrews on 8 November 1762. [SABR]

GLASFORD, ALEXANDER, master of the Jamaica Packet of Burntisland bound for Madeira and Jamaica in 1742. [AJ.224]

GLASFORD, ROBERT, son of bailie Patrick Glasford of Cupar, graduated MA from St Andrews in 1659, minister of Auchterderran from 1689 until deposed in 1690, died in November 1691. [F.V.77]

GLEN, CHRISTIAN, born 1620, died 1687, wife of John Wan in St Fort. [Balmerino gravestone]

GLOVER, JOHN, from Cupar, was admitted as a citizen of Rotterdam, Zealand, on 26 March 1710. [GAR]

GOLLAN, JOHN, a mariner from Dysart, master of the Genoa Merchant probate 1683 Prerogative Court of Canterbury. [TNA]

GOODALE, FRANCIS, a shipmaster in Aberdour, husband of Isobel Wardlaw, born 1700, died 28 March 1763, father of William, born 1724, died in November 1762. [Aberdour St Fillans gravestone]

GOODALE, JOHN, a baker in Auchtermuchty, an inventory, 1759. [NRS.B5.4.1]

GOODSIR, JOHN, a surgeon in Largo, was admitted as a burgess of St Andrews on 6 April 1773. [SABR]

GOODWILLIE, DAVID, schoolmaster of Strathmiglo, 1685. [NRS.RD3.61.629][SHS.4.2]

GOODWILLIE, DAVID, from Cupar, was transported to the colonies in April 1752. [NRS.B59.26.11.5.13]

GORDON, AGNES, Lady Strathvithie, was admitted as a burgess of St Andrews on 3 May 1760. [SABR]

GORDON, ALEXANDER, from Methil, a planter in Jamaica, died there in 1782, testament, 1783, Comm. Edinburgh. [NRS]

GOURLAY, ANDREW, a mariner in Easter Wemyss, testament, 1717, Comm. St Andrews. [NRS]

GOURLAY, DAVID, a sailor in Kinghorn, testament, 1715, Comm. St Andrews. [NRS]

GOURLAY, DAVID, a skipper in Kinghorn, testament, 1754, Comm. St Andrews. [NRS]

GOURLAY, DOUGLAS, a weaver, first son of John Gourlay a weaver in St Andrews, was admitted as a burgess of St Andrews on 12 August 1774. [SABR]

GOURLAY, GEORGE, in Elie, master of the Charles of Anstruther trading with France and Norway in 1670. [NRS.E72.9.4]

GOURLAY, GEORGE, a mariner in Anstruther Easter, testament, 1757, Comm. St Andrews. [NRS]

GOURLAY, JAMES, a weaver in St Andrews, was admitted as a burgess of St Andrews on 2 June 1757. [SABR]

GOURLAY, JOHN, master of the Phoenix of Anstruther trading with Danzig in 1689-1690. [NRS.E72.9.25/27]

GOURLAY, JOHN, a mariner, son of William Gourlay servant to Robert Malcolm in the Grange of Kilconquhar, a testament, 1751, Comm. St Andrews. [NRS]

GOURLAY, JOHN, second son of Robert Gourlay a burgess, was admitted as a burgess of St Andrews 11 March 1755. [SABR]

GOURLAY, JOHN, a weaver, son of William Gourlay the Deacon of the Weavers of St Andrews, was admitted as a burgess of St Andrews on 24 March 1756. [SABR]

GOURLAY, MARTIN, master of the Robert of Elie, a charter party, 1662. [NRS.RD2.5.33; RD4.5.531]

GOURLAY, THOMAS, a mariner in the service of the Honorable East India Company, son of Thomas Gourlay of Balchristy, testament, 1710, Comm. Edinburgh. [NRS]

GOURLAY, WILLIAM, was served heir to his brother Thomas Gourlay of Kincraig, on 22 April 1684. [NRS.Retours.Fife.1237]

GOWAN, JOHN, schoolmaster of Leuchars, 1642. [NRS.GD7.SEC.2.275]

GOWAN, THOMAS, born 1626, a mariner from Dysart, aboard the Negro returning from New England in June 1656. [TNA.HCA.1657]

GRAHAM, JAMES, master of the Peggy of Kirkcaldy trading with North Carolina in 1774-1775. [NRS.E504.20.8][NCSA.S8.112]

GRAHAM, JOHN, a mariner from Burntisland, husband of Euphan Watson, bound for Darien aboard the Endeavour in 1698, testament, 1707, Comm. Edinburgh. [NRS]

GRAHAM, JOHN, a weaver, son of Hugh Graham a weaver burgess, was admitted as a burgess of Dunfermline on 4 July 1797. [DM]

GRAHAM, MUNGO, schoolmaster of Kilrenny, 1690. [SHS.4.2]

GRAY, ANDREW, a meal-maker, first son of James Gray a meal-maker burgess, was admitted as a burgess of St Andrews on 27 December 1774. [SABR]

GRAY, DAVID, from Pittenweem, was admitted as a citizen of Rotterdam on 27 September 1720. [GAR]

GRAY, ELSPETH, relict of James Ireland a mariner burgess of Kirkcaldy, testament, 1718, Comm. St Andrews. [NRS]

GRAY, ISOBEL, wife of Patrick Black the Provost of Dunfermline, was served heir to her father Martin Gray a skipper in Kinghorn on 16 March 1737. [NRS.S/H]

GRAY, JOHN, a councillor of Burntisland in 1689. RPCS.XIV.455]

GRAY, JOHN, minister at Dunfermline from 1688 to 1691. [F.V.29]

GRAY, JOHN, from Creich, a soldier in Georgia, probate 1770, Prerogative Court of Canterbury. [TNA]

GRAY, MARTIN, a mariner in Kinghorn, testament, 1721, Comm. St Andrews. [NRS]

GRAY, ROBERT, a skipper in Anstruther Easter, testament, 1795, Comm. St Andrews. [NRS]

GRAY, THOMAS, a seaman in St Monance, testament, 1635, Comm. St Andrews. [NRS]

GREGORIE, JAMES, master of the David of Wemyss trading between Kirkcaldy and Holland in 1680-1681. [NRS.E72.9/10/13]

GREGORY, WILLIAM, master of the Margaret and Mary of Ferry-Port-on-Craig trading with Christiansand in Norway in 1754. [NRS.E504.27.3]

GREIG, ANDREW, born 1713, tenant in Kelty, died 27 September 1788, husband of Helen Barclay, born 1713, died 24 April 1778. [Beath gravestone]

GREIG, CHARLES, master of the Hope of Inverkeithing bound for South Carolina in 1734. [TNA.CO5.509]; master of the Margaret and Christian of North Queensferry trading with Norway in 1744. [NRS.E504.3.1]

GREIG, HENRY, a skipper in Kirkcaldy, testament, 1707, Comm. St Andrews. [NRS]

GREIG, JAMES, a skipper in Inverkeithing, testament, 1749, Comm. St Andrews. [NRS]

GREIG, JOHN, a skipper in Leven, testament, 1754, Comm. St Andrews. [NRS]

GREIG, JOHN, a merchant, son of John Greig a shipmaster in Dunfermline, was admitted as a burgess of Dunfermline on 19 September 1810. [DM]

GREIG, Sir SAMUEL, born 30 November 1735 in Inverkeithing, son of Captain Charles Greig and his wife Jean Charters, 'father of the Russian Navy', died in Reval on 27 October 1788. [F.5.44][HIR.489]

GREIG, THOMAS, a merchant in Cupar, was admitted as a burgess of St Andrews on 24 October 1761. [SABR]

GREIG, WILLIAM, master of the Dorothea of St Andrews trading with Danzig in 1728.; master of the Helen of St Andrews trading with Spain in 1730. [NRS.CE52.1.3]

GREIG, WILLIAM, a skipper in Burntisland, testament, 1749, Comm. Edinburgh. [NRS]

GRIM, GEORGE, a soldier from Crail, married J. Wauchop in Schiedam in the Netherlands in 1636. [Schiedam Marriage Register]

GROAT, DANIEL, a seaman from Burntisland, son of William Groat, aboard the Unicorn bound for Darien in 1698, testament, 1707, Comm. Edinburgh. [NRS]

GRUBB, Mrs JANET, born 1788 in Fife, was naturalised in New York on 20 May 1828.

GUILLON, ANDREW, a meal-maker in St Andrews, was admitted as a burgess of St Andrews on 28 February 1756. [SABR]

GUILLON, DAVID, in St Andrews, was admitted as a burgess of St Andrews on 8 November 1770. [SABR]

GULLON, WILLIAM, minister at Dunfermline from 1692 to 1694. [F.V.29]

GURLEY, Captain, WILLIAM, of Peterhop, born 1783, settled in St Vincent, died 30 October 1824. [Inverkeithing gravestone]

GUTHRIE, JAMES, a mariner from Largo, aboard the Rising Sun bound for Darien in 1699, died there, testament, 1707, Comm. Edinburgh. [NRS]

GUTHRIE, JAMES, a merchant in Elie, was admitted as a burgess of St Andrews on 21 April 1775. [SABR]

GUTHRIE, SIMON, and his wife Janet Waid in Elie, a deed, 1687. [NRS.GD1.27.16]

HADDIN, DAVID, a shipmaster in Crail, skipper of the Arthur 1643. [SAU.MS36220.389]

HALKERSTON, HOLINUS, of Rathillet, was admitted as a burgess of St Andrews on 5 October 1756. [SABR]

HALKERSTON, JOHN, of Halkerston's Beath, born 1610, died 5 December 1670, husband of Margaret Pearson. [Beath gravestone]

HALKERSTON, ROBERT, son of John Halkerston the clerk of Culross, was apprenticed to James Mitchilson a goldsmith burgess of Edinburgh in 1741. [ERA]

HALKETT, FREDERICK, Lieutenant Colonel of the Scots Brigade, was admitted as a burgess and guilds-brother of Dunfermline on 4 June 1794. [DM]

HALKETT, JOHN, Rector of the Grammar School of Cupar, was admitted as a burgess of St Andrews on 11 September 1755. [SABR]

HALKETT, JOHN, of Pitfirran, born 1769, Governor of the Bahamas, died in 1852. [Dunfermline gravestone]

HALL, JOHN, a merchant in Crail, was admitted as a burgess of St Andrews on 28 March 1758. [SABR]

HALLIDAY, ALEXANDER, a girdle-smith burgess of Culross, a bond, 1720. [NRS.B12.5.1]

HALLOW, STEPHEN, a skipper in Methil, testament, 1753, Comm. St Andrews. [NRS]

HALSON, JOHN, master of the Isabel of Anstruther trading with Danzig, Bergen, and Rotterdam from 1742 to 1765. [NRS.E504.3.1-3]

HALLSON, THOMAS, a mariner in Anstruther, died at sea aboard HMS Plymouth, probate 1692, Prerogative Court of Canterbury. [TNA]

HALSON, WILLIAM, master of the Christian of Anstruther trading with Konigsberg in 1711. [CTB.26.134]; a skipper in Anstruther Easter, testament, 1746, Comm. St Andrews. [NRS]

HALYBURTON, ALEXANDER, was admitted as a burgess and guilds-brother of Dunfermline on 25 September 1792. [DM]

HALYBURTON, JOHN, a skipper in Newburgh, testament, 1798, Comm. St Andrews. [NRS]

HAMILTON, ALEXANDER, a dyer in Linktoun of Abbotshall, his spouse Christian Dewar, a joint grant of the lands and barony of Alloa, by Oliver Cromwell on 21 July 1654. [RGS.X.312]

HAMILTON, GEORGE, a weaver, third son of David Hamilton a guilds-brother of St Andrews, was admitted as a burgess of St Andrews on 7 September 1775. [SABR]

HAMILTON, WILLIAM, a sailor from Crombie, aboard the Unicorn bound for Darien in 1698, testament, 1707, Comm. Edinburgh. [NRS]

HARDIE, JOHN, eldest son of John Hardie, was admitted as a dyer burgess of Auchtermuchty on 31 July 1744. [ABR]

HARDIE, THOMAS, son-in-law of George Hunter a weaver burgess, was admitted a burgess of Dunfermline on 17 September 1790. [DM]

HARLAW, DAVID, a mariner in Pittenweem, 1671. [NRS.RD3.27.411]

HARPER, DAVID, a foremast-man from Kirkcaldy, son of Bessie Salmond or Harper, aboard the Caledonia bound for Darien in 1698, testament, 1707, Comm. Edinburgh. [NRS]

HARRISON, JAMES, a seaman in Burntisland, recruited for service at Port Nelson, Hudson Bay, in March 1683. [HBRS.9.90]

HARROWER, JOHN, son-in-law of John Anderson a tapster in Kirkgate, Dunfermline, was admitted as a burgess of Dunfermline on 19 March 1795. [DM]

HART, JAMES, son-in-law of John Donaldson a burgess, was admitted as a burgess of Dunfermline on 30 April 1801. [DM]

HARVIE, THOMAS, graduated MA from Glasgow University in 1665, minister at Auchterderran from 1692 until 1699. [F.V.77]

HAY, ANDREW, a sailor from Dysart, son of Andrew Hay, aboard the St Andrew bound for Darien in 1698, testament, 1707, Comm. Edinburgh. [NRS]

HAY, ANDREW, an Excise Officer in Anstruther Easter, was admitted as a burgess of St Andrews on 1 April 1758. [SABR]

HAY, ANNA, daughter of Peter Hay of Nauchtane, a bond, 1636. [NRS.GD7.sec.1/40]

HAY, GEORGE, born 1670, a cooper in Fife, foremastman aboard the St Thomas bound for Virginia in 1690. [TNA.HCA.80]

HAY, JAMES, was granted a Crown Charter of the lands of Forret on 24 September 1653. [RGS.X.171]

HAY, JAMES, master of the Euphame and Peggy of Leven trading with Scandinavia in 1761-1763. [NRS.E504.3.3]

HAY, PETER, of Naughton, eldest son of George Hay of Naughton and his wife Margaret Henryson, was granted a Crown Charter in 1662, [RGS.IX.175]; 1694. [BA.633]

HAY, ROBERT, from Dysart, was admitted as a burgess of Bergen, Norway, in 1619. [Bergen City Archives]

HAY, ROBERT, MD in Kirkcaldy, a bond 1731. [NRS.GD26.4.589]

HAYNE, CATHERINE, a widow in Kincapill, testament, 1 August 1598, Comm. St Andrews. [NRS]

HAYNE, JAMES, in Kilmanie, testament, 3 August 1626, Comm. St Andrews. [NRS]

HAYNE, THOMAS, in Balmullo, Leuchars, testament, 3 October 1797, Comm. St Andrews. [NRS]

HEAGIE, JOHN, schoolmaster of Largo, 1690. [SHS.4.2]

HEGGIE, GEORGE, a mariner in Kirkcaldy, testament, 1750, Comm. St Andrews. [NRS]

HEGGIE, JOHN, a mariner in Drumuchie, Largo, husband of Mary Bruce, testament, 1747, Comm. St Andrews. [NRS]

HEGGIE, THOMAS, a skipper in Dysart, husband of Elizabeth Forbes, testament, 1723, Comm. St Andrews. [NRS]

HEGGIE, WILLIAM, schoolmaster of Crail Grammar School, sasine, 1631. [NRS.RS30.9.248]

HEMPSEED, JOHN, son of John Hempseed a baker burgess, was admitted as a burgess of Dunfermline on 20 January 1796. [DM]

HENDERSON, COLIN, a smith in Torryburn, a thief transported aboard the Phoenix bound for Virginia, landed at Port Accomack in 1773. [NRS.JC27][AJ.1293]

HENDERSON, DAVID, a sailor from Burntisland, aboard the Caledonia bound for Darien in 1698, testament, 1707, Comm. Edinburgh. [NRS]

HENDERSON, JAMES, born 1708, son of William Henderson, settled in Augusta County, Virginia, before 1760, died in 1784. [RAV.46]

HENDERSON, JAMES, born 1744, died 27 April 1829, husband of Jean Johnston, born 1749, died 10 February 1821. [Balmerino gravestone]

HENDERSON, JOHN, the younger of Fordell, was admitted as a burgess of St Andrews on 4 June 1765. [SABR]

HENDERSON, JOHN, late from Georgia, in Dunfermline, a sasine, 1787. [NRS.RS31.1635]

HENDERSON, Sir JOHN, of Fordell, was admitted as a burgess and guilds-brother of Dunfermline on 8 April 1791. [DM]

HENDERSON, JOHN, born 1768, son of John Henderson and his wife Elizabeth Hay, a Captain of the 42nd Regiment, [the Black Watch], died in Paullace, France, on 7 July 1814. [Logie gravestone]

HENDERSON, MARGARET, born 1625, died 28 February 1673, wife of James Knox in Peeshills. [Balmerino gravestone]

HENDERSON, THOMAS, a skipper in Inverkeithing, testament, 1756, Comm. Edinburgh. [NRS]

HEPBOURNE, DAVID, daughter [sic], to the deceased William Hepbourne a merchant burgess of Kirkcaldy, a joint grant of the lands and barony of Alloa, by Oliver Cromwell on 21 July 1654. [RGS.X.312]

HERDMAN, ARCHIBALD, a messenger in Dunfermline, son of Archibald Herdman a brewer burgess, was admitted as a burgess of Dunfermline on 17 July 1787. [DM]

HERON, EUPHAME, born 1682, wife of Peter Cunningham smith in Crombie, died 10 September 1755. [Crombie gravestone]

HEWET, ALEXANDER, eldest son of George Hewet a merchant and guilds-brother of St Andrews, was admitted as a burgess of St Andrews on 28 September 1763. [SABR]

HIRD, WILLIAM, son of William Hird, a physician in Rennes, Brittany, France, 1626. [NRS.S/H.1626]

HODGE, WILLIAM, a merchant in Anstruther, was admitted as a burgess of St Andrews on 12 September 1761. [SABR]

HOG, ALEXANDER, born 1684, feuar in Lochgelly, died 25 May 1748, husband of Grizel Hog, born 1662, died 8 March 1734. [Beath gravestone]

HOGG, GAVIN, factor to Sir John Anstruther of that Ilk, was admitted as a burgess of St Andrews on 4 July 1760. [SABR]

HOGG, JAMES, a merchant in Anstruther, was admitted as a burgess of St Andrews on 26 September 1765. [SABR]

HOG, JAMES, son of Peter Hog a weaver burgess, was admitted as a burgess of Dunfermline on 25 July 1796. [DM]

HOGAN, WILLIAM, a mariner from Kinghorn, before the Scots Court in Veere, Zealand, in 1735. [NRS.RH11.2]

HONEYMAN, DAVID, in the Grange of Balmerino in 1717. [BA.634]

HONEYMAN, THOMAS, a baker, second son of Thomas Honeyman the Deacon of the Bakers of St Andrews, was admitted as a burgess of St Andrews on 8 September 1773. [SABR]

HONEYMAN, WILLIAM, in Grange Balfour, Balmerino, in 1694. [BA.632]

HOOD, MARTIN, a soldier from Burntisland, married Annette Antonis in Brielle, the Netherlands in 1681. [Brielle Marriage Register]

HOPE, CHARLES, servant to Wemyss of Unthank, was admitted as a burgess of St Andrews on 17 October 1759. [SABR]

HOPE, JOHN, a land-surveyor in Falkland, a report, 1790. [NRS.GD1.675.17]

HOPE, Sir WILLIAM, was served heir to his father Sir Thomas Hope of Craighall on 21 September 1686. [NRS.Retours. Fife.1272]

HORSBURGH, DAVID, a tailor in Crail, heir to his father James Horsburgh a wright burgess of Crail, 1763. [NRS.B10.5.1/44]

HORSBURGH, JAMES, born 23 September 1792 in Elie, the Honorable East India Company Hydrographer in Bombay, India, died 14 May 1836. [Elie gravestone]

HORSBURGH, JOHN, was admitted as a shoemaker burgess of Crail in 1790. [CBR]

HORSBURGH, LAURENCE, elder son of John Horsburgh a guilds-brother of St Andrews, was admitted as a burgess of St Andrews on 18 June 1772. [SABR]

HORSBURGH, PHILIP, elder son of George Horsburgh a guilds-brother of St Andrews, was admitted as a burgess of St Andrews on 18 June 1772. [SABR]

HORSBURGH, THOMAS, master of the Helen of Pittenweem trading with Bremen, Germany, in 1742. [NRS.E504.3.1]

HORSBURGH, WILLIAM, master of the Helen of Pittenweem trading with Christiansands, Norway, in 1762. [NRS.E504.3.3]

HOUSTOUN, ALEXANDER, schoolmaster of Kilconquhar, 1690. [SHS.4.2]

HOWDEN, JOHN, born 1783, son of Archibald Howden and his wife Joan Manderson, a merchant, died in Savannah, Georgia, on 26 October 1806. [St Monance gravestone][Savannah Death Register]

HOY, GEORGE, born 1776, died 1 January 1796. [Culross Abbey gravestone]

HOY, JAMES, a burgess of Newburgh by 1740. [NBR]

HUNT, JOHN, from Dunfermline, settled in Charleston, South Carolina, in 1803, naturalised there in 1808. [South Carolina Court of Common Pleas, Z3/150]

HUNTER, DAVID, born 1731, died 25 December 1791, husband of Betty Tilles, born 1743, died 16 June 1813, [Burntisland, St Columba's, gravestone]

HUNTER, MARGARET, in Culross, sister of James Hunter a carpenter in Jamaica, a discharge to David Gellatly a merchant in Jamaica, 1798. [NRS.B12.5.4]

HUNTER, ROBERT, miller of Shaw's Mill, Auchtertool, a tack, 1697. [NRS.GD26.5.87]

HUTCHISON, ANDREW, born 1786, son of Andrew Hutchison and his wife Mary Malcolm, surgeon aboard HMS Sapphire, died at Chagre on the Spanish Main, on 17 September 1819. [Burntisland gravestone]

HUTCHISON, DAVID, born 1726, died in May 1798, husband of Margaret Drysdale who died 17 March 1773. [Culross Abbey gravestone]

HUTTON, DAVID, a skinner burgess of Dysart, husband of Marion Dyne, a deed, 1695. [NRS.B21.5.1/9]

HUTTON, JAMES, schoolmaster of Carnock, 1682. [NRS.RD4.50.1]

HUTTON, JAMES, a meal-maker in Denhead, was admitted as a burgess of St Andrews on 9 May 1765. [SABR]

HUTTON, JAMES, born 1747 in Fife, a factor who was naturalised in Charleston, South Carolina, in 1796. [NARA.M1183/1]

HUTTON, ROBERT, a mason in Pitdinny, was admitted as a burgess of Dunfermline on 17 February 1789. [DM]

IMRIE, JAMES, a baker in Inverkeithing, son of John Imrie a butcher burgess of Dunfermline, was admitted as a burgess of Dunfermline on 22 September 1807. [DM]

IMRIE, JOHN, born 1636, died 1716. [Ferry-Port-on-Craig gravestone]

IMRIE, JOHN, a shipbuilder in Ferry-Port-on-Craig, later in Dundee, a deed, 1791. [NRS.SC20.36.15]

IMRIE, PATRICK, a carpenter and sailor in Cellardyke, testament, 1750, Comm. St Andrews. [NRS]

IMRIE, THOMAS, in Scotscraig, born 1567, died on 15 April 1642. [Ferry-Port-on-Craig gravestone]

IMRIE, WILLIAM, in Flisk, and his wife Janet Swantoun daughter of the deceased John Swantoun in Grange, were granted property at Kinloch, Collessie, on 24 December 1658. [RGS.X.671]

INCH, DAVID, tenant in Gallowhill, was admitted as a burgess and guilds-brother of Dunfermline on 26 September 1791. [DM]

INGLES, ANDREW, the Sheriff Substitute of Fife, was admitted as a burgess and guilds-brother of Dunfermline on 9 August 1786. [DM]

INGLIS, CHARLES, a sailor from St Andrews, son of James Inglis, board the Rising Sun bound for Darien in 1699, testament, 1707, Comm. Edinburgh. [NRS]

INGLIS, DAVID, a skipper in Inverkeithing, master of the Adam and Betty of Inverkeithing bound for Jamaica in 1763, and to Grenada in 1764, of the Expedition of Inverkeithing bound for Grenada in 1765, [NRS.E504.22.11/12]; testament, 1767, Comm. Edinburgh. [NRS]

INGLIS, DAVID, a skipper in Inverkeithing, testament, 1783, Comm. St Andrews. [NRS]

INGLIS, GEORGE, a journeyman shoemaker in Cupar, versus Katherine Rodgers daughter of Alexander Rodgers a shoemaker in Kennoway who married in April 1769, Process of Divorce, 27 April 1773. [NRS.CC8.6.523]

INGLIS, HENRY, a sailor from Kinghorn, aboard the St Andrew bound for Darien in 1698, testament, 1707, Comm. Edinburgh. [NRS]

INGLIS, JAMES, minister at Burntisland from 1693 until 1699. [F.V.82]

INGLIS, ROBERT, a sailor from St Andrews, died on the Rising Sun at Darien, Panama, in 1699, testament, 1707, Comm. Edinburgh. [NRS]

INGLIS, ROBERT, a skipper in Kinghorn, testament, 1754, Comm. St Andrews. [NRS]

INNES, DAVID, a weaver in Cupar, was admitted as a burgess of St Andrews in 1774. [SABR]

INNES, JOHN, of Leuchars, a Captain of the Royal American Regiment, versus Elizabeth Gordon, a decreet in abstentia, 8 December 1756. [NRS.CS16.1.99/116]

INNES, JOHN, a skipper in St Monance, testament, 1800, Comm. St Andrews. [NRS]

INNES, ROBERT, a widower from Leuchars, died in Newark, Nottinghamshire, probate, 1650. PCC. [TNA]

INNES, WILLIAM, born 1747, the parochial school-master of Forgan, died 8 September 1823. [Fife Herald]

INSTANT, ROBERT, son of David Instant in Pittenweem, a mariner aboard the Welcome, died at sea, probate, 1686, PCC. [TNA]

INVERARITY, JAMES, master of the Success of St Andrews trading with Danzig in 1770. [NRS.E504.3.4]

IRELAND, JOHN, born 1717, died 16 January 1793, his wife Margaret Colvell, born 1728, died 12 November 1794. [Ferry-Port-on-Craig gravestone]

IRELAND, WILLIAM, son of Robert Ireland a merchant burgess, was admitted as a burgess of Dunfermline on 11 April 1788. [DM]

IRVINE, JOHN, an English teacher in Cupar, was admitted as a burgess of St Andrews on 8 June 1765. [SABR]

ISAAC, ALEXANDER, a sailor from Tulliallan, aboard the Unicorn bound for Darien in 1698, testament, 1707, Comm. Edinburgh. [NRS]

IZETT, JOHN, a candle-maker in Kirkcaldy, a deed, 1764. [NRS.B21.5.2/7]

JACK, DAVID WILLIAM, born 25 February 1785, son of William Jack in Cupar, settled in St Andrews, New Brunswick. [American Armory and Blue Book, London, 1903]

JACKSON, JAMES, schoolmaster of Dunbog, 1690. [SHS.4.2]

JAMIESON, CHRISTIAN, spouse to Thomas Selcraig in Largo, testament, 1614, Comm. St Andrews. [NRS]

JAMIESON, FRANCIS, a weaver in Pittencrieff, former apprentice to Andrew Stevenson a weaver burgess, was admitted as a burgess of Dunfermline on 25 March 1790. [DM]

JAMIESON, JAMES, a sailor from Burntisland, son of James Jackson, aboard the Unicorn bound for Darien in 1698, testament, 1707, Comm. Edinburgh. [NRS]

JAMIESON, THOMAS, a druggist in Dunfermline, was admitted as a burgess and guilds-brother of Dunfermline on 7 September 1789. [DM]

JAMIESON, WILLIAM, a weaver burgess of Crail, heir to his father John Jamieson a weaver burgess of Crail, 1776. [NRS.B10.5.1/95]

JOHNSON, THOMAS, from Anstruther, was admitted as a burgess of Bergen, Norway, in 1627. [Bergen City Archives]

JOHNSTON, ANDREW, a merchant in Anstruther, was admitted as a burgess of St Andrews on 6 January 1769. [SABR]

JOHNSTON, ANDREW, son of James Johnston a weaver burgess, was admitted as a burgess of Dunfermline on 27 July 1789. [DM]

JOHNSTON, GEORGE, born 1643, graduated MA from Edinburgh University in 1659, minister at Burntisland from 1688 until 1691, died 20 February 1729. [F.V.82]

JOHNSTON, GRIZEL, born 1737, spouse of John Elder, died 11 March 1779. [Auchtermuchty gravestone]

JOHNSTON, HENRY, from the Hill of Kirkcaldy, former master of a Dutch ship, 1708. [NRS.AC10.68]

JOHNSTON, JOHN, son of a maltman in Culross, a prisoner in Edinburgh Tolbooth, to Holland as a soldier under Captain Thomas Hamilton on 11 March 1684. [RPCS.3.8.403/683]

JOHNSTON, ROBERT, minister of Aberdour in 1689. [F.V.3]

JOHNSTON, SAMUEL, born 1722, tenant in Little Inch, died 27 November 1803, husband of Ann Mitchell, born 1730, died 4 January 1802. [Balmerino gravestone]

JOHNSTON, WALTER, a sailor in St Andrews, testament, 1712, Comm. St Andrews. [NRS]

JOHNSTON, WALTER, a skipper in West Wemyss, testament, 1754, Comm. St Andrews. [NRS]

JOHNSTON, WILLIAM WILLIAMSON, from Dysart, was admitted as a burgess of Bergen, Norway, in 1626. [Bergen City Archives]

JOHNSTON, WILLIAM, master of the John of Crail trading with Melstrand in 1689. [NRS.E72.9.24]

JOHNSTON, WILLIAM, schoolmaster of Dalgetty, 1690. [SHS.4.2]

JONES, WILLIAM, master of the St David of Dysart trading with Philadelphia before 1742. [NRS.AC9.1487]

JUST, DAVID, of Justfield, born 1714, a mason, died in June 1794, husband of Ann Medseo, born 1712, died 24 March 1772. [Forgan gravestone]

JUST, RANALD, in Sea Mylne, Forgan, testament, 1 December 1613, Comm. St Andrews. [NRS]

JUST, THOMAS, of Justfield, born 1741, died 8 January 1821, wife [1] Jean Simson, born 1741, died in July 1809, wife [2] Barbara Mackie, born 1775, died 8 December 1855. [Forgan gravestone]

JUSTICE, JAMES, was admitted as a brewer burgess of Auchtermuchty on 25 January 1751. [ABR]

KAY, ROBERT, minister at Dunfermline from 1645 until 1665. [F.V.28]

KAY, WILLIAM, a skipper in South Ferry, testament, 1804, Comm. St Andrews. [NRS]

KEADY, DAVID, a skipper from Leven, an assessor of the Scots Court at Veere, Zealand, 1739. [NRS.RH11.2]; master of the George of Kinghorn trading with Gothenburg in 1742. [NRS.E504.3.1]

KELLOCK, GEORGE, son of George Kellock a shoemaker burgess, was admitted as a burgess of Dunfermline on 17 August 1792. [DM]

KELLOCK, MICHAEL, in Burntisland, a charter witness, 21 July 1654. [RGS.X.311]

KELLY, JOHN, in St Andrews, was admitted as a burgess of St Andrews on 20 December 1762. [SABR]

KELTIE, JOHN, 'pretended' baillie of Auchtermuchty, 1784. [NRS.CS228.A5.23]

KELTIE, JOHN, a weaver, son of James Keltie a burgess, was admitted as a burgess of Dunfermline on 4 July 1797. [DM]

KEMP, HUGH, minister at Dunfermline from 1701 to 1704. [F.V.29]

KEMP, JAMES, a skipper in South Ferry of Portincraig, testament, 16 April 1627, Comm. St Andrews. [NRS]

KENNEDY, ANDREW, and his spouse Margaret Bruce, in Kinghorn, a deed, 1635. [NRS.B9.14.32]

KENNEDY, DAVID, born in 1773, son of Thomas Kennedy and his wife Ann Gibb in Falkland, a merchant in Philadelphia, died in Germantown, Pennsylvania, in 1798. [Falkland gravestone]

KENNEDY, PETER, schoolmaster of Dunfermline Grammar School, testament, 6 February 1705, Comm. St Andrews. [NRS]

KENNELL, JAMES, a weaver, son-in-law of James Anderson a weaver burgess, was admitted as a burgess of Dunfermline on 16 September 1803. [DM]

KENT, JOHN, a skipper in Burntisland, husband of Marion Harper, testament, 1621, Comm. St Andrews. [NRS]

KERMUCK, DAVID, schoolmaster in Ceres, was admitted as a burgess of St Andrews on 5 October 1762. [SABR]

KERR, ALEXANDER, schoolmaster of Kirkcaldy, 1683. [NRS.RD2.61.137]

KER, THOMAS, heir to his father Thomas Ker the minister at Balmerino, 6 April 1745. [NRS.S/H]

KER, THOMAS, the minister at Balmerino, and Margaret Oliphant, eldest daughter of George Oliphant of Prinlaws, a marriage contract, 1726. [NRS.SC20.26.7]

KETTLE, THOMAS YOUNG, born 27 November 1778 in Leuchars, son of Reverend Thomas Kettle and his wife Sarah Young, settled in Savannah, Georgia. [F.5.222]

KEY, ANDREW, the elder, a carpenter in Ferry-Port-on-Craig, and Nicola Gregory, daughter of John Gregory in Ferry-Port-on-Craig, a marriage contract, 1727. [NRS.SC20.33.11]

KEY, DAVID, master of the Margaret of Ferry-Port-on-Craig trading with Bordeaux in 1726. [NRS.CE52.4.1]

KEY, DAVID, a skipper in Ferry-Port-on-Craig, a deed, 1791. [NRS.SC20.36.15]

KEY, HELEN, relict of Alexander Duncan a land labourer in Ferry-Port-on-Craig, a deed, 1791. [NRS.SC20.36.15]

KEY, KATHERINE, in Ferry-Port-on-Craig, testament, 23 July 1712, Comm. St Andrews. [NRS]

KEY, JOHN, second son of Thomas Key a meal-maker burgess of St Andrews, was admitted as a burgess of St Andrews on 26 December 1772. [SABR]

KEY, ROBERT, son of Thomas Key late minister of Kilrenny, was admitted as a burgess of St Andrews on 25 June 1759. [SABR]

KEY, THOMAS, elder son of Thomas Key a meal-maker burgess of St Andrews, was admitted as a burgess of St Andrews on 26 December 1772. [SABR]

KEY, WALTER, a merchant from Kirkcaldy, an assessor of the Scots Court in Zealand in 1728. [NRS.RH11.2]

KEY, WILLIAM, a skipper and carpenter in Ferry-Port-on-Craig, testament, 1774, Comm. St Andrews. [NRS]

KID, JAMES, born 1756, died 4 June 1821, wife Elspeth Greig, son David, born 1790, died 12 November 1790, son James, born 1792, died 2 April 1820. [Forgan gravestone]

KID, WILLIAM, mariner in Ferry-Port-on-Craig, and his wife Eupham Smyth, a sasine, 1605. [NRS.RS30.VII.9]

KILGOUR, ALEXANDER, a sailor from Lochgelly, aboard the Caledonia bound for Darien in 1698, testament, 1709, Comm. Edinburgh. [NRS]

KILGOUR, GEORGE, schoolmaster of St Andrews, husband of Catherine Balbirnie, testament, 13 June 1674, Comm. St Andrews. [NRS][NRS.RD4.37.577]

KILGOUR, RICHARD, a weaver, son of David Kilgour a smith burgess, was admitted as a burgess of Dunfermline on 27 September 1790. [DM]

KILGOUR, WILLIAM, a mariner in Leven, a sasine, 1720.
[NRS.RS.Fife.115.228]

KILPATRICK, DAVID, son of David Kilpatrick the younger a weaver
burgess, was admitted as a burgess of Dunfermline on 28
November 1792. [DM]

KING, JAMES, born 1797, son of James King and his wife Helen
Skinner, a vine grower in New South Wales, died in London on 29
November 1857. [Kinconquhar gravestone]

KING, MITCHELL, born 1783 in Crail, emigrated to America in
1805, a teacher and judge in Charleston, South Carolina,
naturalised there in 1810, died 1862. [NARA.M1183/1]

KINGO, JAMES, Convenor of the Trades of Crail, was admitted as
a burgess of St Andrews on 27 February 1758, [SABR]; a deed,
1773. [NRS.B10.5.1/80]

KINGO, JOHN, was admitted as a weaver burgess of Crail in 1783.
[CBR]

KINLOCH, DAVID, master of the Bachelor of Dysart trading with
Rotterdam in 1726. [NRS.CE52.1.3]

KINLOCH, GEORGE, schoolmaster of Falkland, 1670.
[NRS.RD4.27.667]

KINLOCH, JOHN, son of David Kinloch a burgess, was admitted as
a burgess of Dunfermline on 3 August 1802. [DM]

KINLOCH, ROBERT, schoolmaster of Falkland, 1646-1653.
[SAU.msRossie 5/650]

KINNAIRD, JAMES, a sailor in Crail, testament, 1755, Comm. St
Andrews. [NRS]

KINNEAR, CHRISTOPHER, born 1794 in Dysart, emigrated to Halifax, Nova Scotia, died in Baltimore, Maryland, on 26 September 1821. [Free Press 13.11.1821]

KINNEAR, DAVID, a hammerman in Dunnikier, a deed in favour of his grandson David Kinnear eldest son of George Kinnear a smith there, a deed, 1731. [NRS.RH11.27.36/18]

KINNELL, JOHN, a mariner in Kinghorn, testament, 1710, Comm. Edinburgh. [NRS]

KINNINMONTH, ANDREW, a seaman in Aberdour, husband of Marie Bell, daughter of Archibald Bell a maltman in Aberdour, a sasine 1680. [NRS.GD1.127.7]

KINNINMONTH, Captain DAVID, was granted various lands in Fife by Oliver Cromwell the Lord Protector on 14 July 1654. [RGS.X.307]

KINNINMONT, JOHN, born 1769, husband of Catherine Carstairs, died 1815 in France. [Kilconquhar gravestone]

KINNINMONTH, THOMAS, MA St Andrews in 1657, minister at Auchterderran from 1668 until his death in July 1687, husband of Catherine Forrester. [F.V.76]

KIRK, ARCHIBALD, born 1656, a burgess of Culross, died 6 December 1717. [Culross West gravestone]

KIRK, DOUGAL, son of Charles Kirk a smith burgess, was admitted as a burgess of Kirkcaldy on 24 September 1793. [DM]

KIRK, GEORGE, a wright, son of George Kirk a meal-maker, was admitted as a burgess of St Andrews on 11 September 1761. [SABR]

KIRK, GEORGE, in St Andrews in 1798. [NRS.E326.15.31]

KIRKCALDY, THOMAS, son of Thomas Kirkcaldy a guilds-brother, was admitted as a burgess of Dunfermline on 9 July 1799. [DM]

KIRKLAND, JOHN, a baker, was admitted as a burgess of Dunfermline on 29 June 1798. [DM]

KNOX, JAMES, schoolmaster of Falkland, 1701. [SAU, Rossie ms 11/150]

KYD, GEORGE, son of Captain Kyd in Elie, a physician who died on St Vincent in 1775. [SM.37.286]

KYD, Captain JAMES, master of the Princess Anne, was admitted as a burgess of St Andrews n 5 October 1756. [SABR]

LAING, DAVID, born 1741, died in Lindores on 3 April 1802, husband of Margaret Wilkie, born 1747, died 8 August 1831. [Abdie gravestone]

LAING, JAMES, a merchant in Culross, a bond, 1724. [NRS.BB12.5.1/109]

LAING, JAMES, born 1765, a merchant in Auchtermuchty, died 23 August 1825. [Auchtermuchty gravestone]

LAING, or CLARK, JEAN, born 1731, died 18 January 1807. [St Andrews gravestone]

LAING, JOHN, a burgess of Newburgh by 1740. [NBR]

LAING, PATRICK, schoolmaster of Grange, 1668. [SUL. Rossie ms 11/48]

LAING, PETER, a draper in Newburgh, settled at the Cape of Good Hope, died 1813. [Abdie gravestone]

LAMB, PITCAIRN, a seaman in Pittenweem, 1787. [NRS.B3.7.5]

LAMB, THOMAS, born 1729 in Fife, a merchant in Charleston, South Carolina, died 1786. [Old Scots gravestone, Charleston]

LAMOND, JOHN, a sailor from Kincardine-on-Forth, aboard the Endeavour bound for Darien in 1698, testament, 1707, Comm. Edinburgh. [NRS]

LAMONT, JAMES, a skipper in Elie, husband of Mary Lundin testament, 1751, Comm. St Andrews. [NRS]

LAMONT, NEIL, MD, from Fife, a member of the Scots Charitable Society of Boston, New England, in 1758. [NEHGS]

LAMONTH, ALAN, schoolmaster of Dysart Grammar School, husband of Isabel Clark, 16... [NRS.RS30.1.123]

LANDALE, ALEXANDER, master of the Margaret of Leven trading with Norway in 1749. [NRS.E504.3.2]

LANDALE, ANDREW, a skipper in Leven, later in St Andrews, testament, 1780, Comm. St Andrews. [NRS]; master of the Alexander and James of Anstruther trading with Danzig in 1744. [NRS.E504.3.1]

LANDALE, ANDREW, of Pitmeddan, born 1757, died 20 October 1824, husband of Janet Fleming, born 1762, died 25 May 1826. [Auchtermuchty gravestone]

LANDALE, JOHN, master of the Elizabeth of Leven trading with Rotterdam in 1767. [NRS.E504.27.3]

LANDELS, MARGARET, was served heir to her father Henry Landels in Boggie, on 21 October 1687. [NRS.Retours.Fife.1285]

LATHANGIE, HENRY, portioner of Ballangall, husband of Jean Glas, a sasine, 1617. [NRS.RS31.I.195]

LAUCHLIN, JOSEPH, a meal-maker in St Andrews, was admitted as a burgess of St Andrews on 28 February 1756. [SABR]

LAVEROCK, DAVID, in Buckhaven, husband of Janet Elistone, a sasine, 16 29. [NRS.RS31.VIII.83]

LAW, ALEXANDER, a burgess of Kirkcaldy, was served heir to his brother german James Law son of James Law, late Provost of Kirkcaldy, on 8 January 1692. [NRS.Retours.Fife.1329]

LAW, DAVID, born 1675, a maltman and a bailie of Culross, died 13 November 1757. [Culross Abbey gravestone]

LAW, JAMES, a meal-maker in St Andrews, was admitted as a burgess of St Andrews on 17 December 1771. [SABR]

LAW, ROBERT, master of the Blessing of Anstruther trading with Stockholm in 1626. [RPCS.I.435]

LAW, ROBERT, of Cameron, a merchant in St Andrews, a deed, 1706. [NRS.RD3.111.69]

LAW, THOMAS, a lace-maker from Anstruther, was admitted as a citizen of Danzig in 1634. [SIG.203]

LAW, WILLIAM, a foremast-man from Kirkcaldy, aboard the Caledonia bound for Darien in 1698, testament, 1707, Comm. Edinburgh. [NRS]

LAW, WILLIAM, a skipper in Burntisland, testament, 1808, Comm. St Andrews. [NRS]

LAWRENCE, DAVID, a baillie of Culross, was admitted as a burgess and guilds-brother of Dunfermline on 3 July 1790. [DM]

LAWRIE, ALEXANDER, schoolmaster of Falkland, 1690. [SHS.4.2]

LAWRIE, DAVID, son of David Lawrie a soap-boiler burgess, was admitted as a burgess of Dunfermline on 23 September 1802. [DM]

LAWSON, ALEXANDER, a writer in Falkland, a bond, 4 September 1691. [NRS.PC12.16.110]

LAWSON, DAVID, schoolmaster of Torryburn, 1690. [SHS.4.2]

LAWSON, DAVID, born 1778 in Fife, a blacksmith in the parish of Kingston, King's County, New Brunswick, was drowned on 10 June 1804. [St John Gazette: 18.6.1804]

LAWSON, ELIZABETH, relict of William Anderson a skipper, parents of James Anderson, a bond, 21 January 1749. [NRS.GD7.SEC1.64]

LAWSON, JAMES, a merchant in Anstruther, account book, 1688-1698, [NRS.CS25/17.12.1714]

LAWSON, JEAN, relict of John Greig a skipper in Leven, testament, 1754, Comm. St Andrews. [NRS]

LAWSON, PETER, a weaver in Torryburn, a thief transported aboard the Phoenix to Virginia, landed at Port Accomack in 1773. [NRS.JC27.10.3][AJ.1293]

LAWSON, ROBERT, master of the Charming Betty of Anstruther trading with Danzig in 1743. [NRS.E504.3.3]

LAWTHRISK, DAVID, in Meikle Balquhumrie, husband of Grisel Forrester, a sasine, 1630. [NRS.RS31.VIII.462]

LEARMONTH, GEORGE, of Balcomie, a sasine, 1620. [NRS.RS31.III.42]

LEARMONTH, JAMES, of Dairsie, Provost of St Andrews, a sasine, 1621. [NRS.RS31.III.359]

LEE, JAMES, from St Andrews, husband of Mary Crookshank, parents of James, settled in New York, died there on 9 October 1795. [ANY.2.83]

LEES, HENRY, from Kirkcaldy, a gunner aboard the Lion of Zeeland in 1631, [ZA]

LEGAT, JAMES, a merchant in Dunfermline, husband of Margaret Stirk, a sasine, 1630. [NRS.RS31.VIII.385]

LEIPER, THOMAS, a merchant from St Andrews, in Konigsberg in 1617. [SAU.HL.726]

LEITCH, DAVID, of Moonzie Mill, husband of Eupham Inglis, a sasine, 1623. [NRS.RS31.IV.368]

LEITH, DAVID, nephew of David Wilson, a sasine, 1617. [NRS.RS31.I.253]

LEITH, ROBERT, a former bailie of Pittenweem, settled in Philadelphia before 1751. [NRS.CS16.1.85]

LENNOX, JAMES, in Leuchars, husband of Elizabeth Loutfoote, a sasine, 1635. [NRS.RS31.XI.289]

LENNOX, JAMES, of Broombrae, born 1713, died 17 January 1763. [Auchtermuchty gravestone]

LENNOX, JOHN, a 'messer' in St Andrews, testament, 1701.Comm. St Andrews. [NRS]

LENNOX, WILLIAM, a mariner in Crail, testament, 1716, Comm. St Andrews. [NRS]

LENTRON, DAVID, a skipper in St Andrews, a sasine, 1628. [NRS.RS31.VIII.349]

LENTRON, PATRICK, a bailie of St Andrews, a sasine, 1652. [NRS.RS31.XVIII.388]

LERMONTH, Sir JAMES, of Balcomy, Crail, subscribed to charters dated 24 October 1634, and 3 June 1650. [RGS.X.173]

LESLIE, Sir ALEXANDER, later Earl of Leven, born 1582, son of George Leslie, a Captain in the Dutch-Spanish War of 1605, a Swedish Army officer from 1608 to 1638, returned to Scotland in

1638, led the Covenanter invasion of England in 1639, died 1661 in Balgonie. [NRS.GD26.3.2.215-221][SHR.IX.40]

LESLIE, Colonel ALEXANDER, son of Sir Alexander Leslie of Balgonie, General of the Armies of Scotland, a sasine, 1651. [NRS.RS31.XIII.38]

LESLIE, ALEXANDER, servant of Sir John Anstruther, was admitted as a burgess of St Andrews on 30 September 1765. [SABR]

LESLIE, ALEXANDER, born 1765, son of Andrew Leslie and his wife Jean Orrock, died 1816 in America. [Burntisland gravestone]

LESLIE, ALEXANDER, born 1767 in Fife, a farmer who settled in Richmond, Virginia, naturalised in Virginia in 1799. [US.D/C.1799.34]

LESLY, ANDREW, graduated MA from St Andrews in 1625, minister at Burntisland from 1640 until his death on 4 April 1643. [F.V.81]

LESLIE, ANDREW, schoolmaster of Newburn, and later Elie, deed, 1667, [NRS.RD4.18.884]; testament, 25 January 1683, Comm. St Andrews. [NRS]

LESLIE, DAVID, from Kirkcaldy, died aboard HMS Vanguard probate 1692, PCC. [TNA]

LESLIE, JOHN, a soldier from Kirkcaldy, married Belijtgie van Maaseyck in Schiedam, the Netherlands, in 1632. [Schiedam Marriage Register]

LESLIE, JOHN, born 1772, son of Andrew Leslie and his wife Jean Orrock, died 1818 in America. [Burntisland gravestone]

LESLIE, JOHN, a police officer in Dunfermline, was admitted as a burgess of Dunfermline on 17 August 1783. [DM]

LESLIE, MARY, Lady Drumcarrow, St Andrews, mother of William Ayton, a deed, 1715. [NRS.RD4.116.959]

LESLIE, THOMAS, the younger, a merchant in St Andrews, son of Thomas Leslie of Riggs, a deed, 1715. [NRS.RD3.146.569]

LESSELLS, JAMES, was admitted as a sloop-master burgess of Crail in 1801. [CBR]

LESSELLS, JOHN, a land labourer in St Andrews, testament, 1724, Comm. St Andrews. [NRS]

LESSELLS, JOHN, a skipper in Cellardyke, 1741. [NRS.B3.7.2]

LESSLY, ANDREW, from Fife, a member of the Scots Charitable Society of Boston, New England, in 1752. [NEHGS]

LIDDELL, JAMES, born 1798, son of James Liddell and his wife Agnes Leighton, a Major of the 1st Bombay Cavalry, died in Kotra on 3 June 1841. [Aberdour gravestone]

LIES, DAVID, in Pittenweem, a deed, 1687. [NRS.GD62.228]

LIGHTON, PATRICK, a seaman from Burntisland, son of Robert Lighton and his wife Christian Hay, aboard the Rising Sun bound for Darien in 1699, testament, 1707, Comm. Edinburgh. [NRS]

LILBURNE, JOHN, a mariner from Kirkcaldy, died at sea, probate 1658, PCC. [TNA]

LINDSAY, ADAM, of Nativity, born 1754, a Lieutenant Colonel of the 7th Bengal Native Infantry in the service of the Honorable East India Company, died 12 March 1812. [Dunfermline gravestone]

LINDSAY, ALEXANDER, born 1610 in Dysart, emigrated via Amsterdam aboard the Harinck bound for the New Netherlands in 1639, with his wife Catherine Duncanson, settled at Fort

Nassau, later at Fort Orange, died 13 November 1685.
[DP][NWI.I.119]

LINDSAY, GEORGE, born 1737, son of George Lindsay of
Wormiston and his wife Margaret Bethune, a writer who died in
Havanna, Cuba, in 1762. [SP.5.415]

LINDSAY, JAMES, born 1794, son of John Lindsay and his wife
Margaret Jackson, a joiner who died in New Orleans on 28 August
1822. [Falkland gravestone]

LINDSAY, JOHN, born 2 July 1694 in Crail, son of John Lindsay and
his wife Margaret Haliburton, a merchant who settled in New
York after 1729, died in Albany, New York, on 12 October 1751.
[HSBC][N.Y.Col.ms72/170][SP.5.415][NRS.203]

LINDSAY, Master JOHN, was served heir to his grand-father
Master John Lindsay of Wormeston on 26 July 1692.
[NRS.Retours.Fife.1335]

LINDSAY, JOHN, of Wormiston, was admitted as a burgess of St
Andrews on 2 June 1766. [SABR]

LINDSAY, PATRICK, schoolmaster of St Andrews, 1690. [SHS.4.2]

LINDSAY, PETER, born 1700, son of John Lindsay of Wormiston,
Crail, a Jacobite in 1745. [SHS.8.66/374]

LINDSAY, ROBERT, schoolmaster of Drumedrie, Newburn, deed,
1679, [NRS.RD2.48.588]; 1690. [SHS.4.2]

LINDSAY, THOMAS, in St Andrews, was admitted as a burgess of
St Andrews on 29 July 1760. [SABR]

LINDSAY, WILLIAM, minister at Auchterderran from 1663 until
1668. [F.V.76]

LINDSAY, WILLIAM, a skipper in Methil, testament, 1780, Comm.
St Andrews. [NRS]

LINDESAY, WILLIAM, of Feddinch, born 1728, died 1 June 1803. [St Andrews gravestone]

LITHILL, DAVID, schoolmaster of Kingsbarns, 1690. [SHS.4.2]

LITSTER, HUGH, born 1678, son of Reverend Thomas Litster and his wife Margaret Lindsay in Aberdour, a sailor aboard the Rising Sun, participated in the Darien Expedition, died in Charleston, South Carolina, in 1699, testament, 1708, Comm. Edinburgh. [NRS][F.5.3]

LITSTER, JAMES, schoolmaster of Aberdour, 1690. [SHS.4.2]

LITSTER, THOMAS, graduated MA from St Andrews in 1656, a schoolmaster from 1662, minister at Auchtertool from 1665 to 1668, then minister of Aberdour from 1668 until his death in June 1689, husband of Margaret Lindsay, parents of James, Katherine, William, Anna, Margaret, Hugh, Thomas, Margaret, Helen, and James. [F.V.3/78]

LITTLEJOHN, ALEXANDER, a notary public and town-clerk of Ferry-Port-on-Craig, sasines, 1605-1608. [NRS.RS30.V.225/XI.229]

LIVINGSTONE, ELIZABETH, relict of Patrick Cairns in St Andrews, a bond, 1707. [NRS.B65.5.2/30]

LIVINGSTONE, JAMES, son of Andrew Livingstone, bailie of Strathmiglo, a deed, 1715. [NRS.RD3.144.393]

LIVINGSTON, JAMES, a burgess of Newburgh by 1740. [NBR]

LIVINGSTONE, RICHARD, a burgess of Strathmiglo, husband of Margaret Duncan, a sasine, 1638,   [NRS.RS31.XXII.110]

LIVINGSTON, WILLIAM, graduated MA from St Andrews in 1631, minister at Burntisland from 1663 until 1672. [F.V.82]

LOCH, DAVID, master of the Providence of Anstruther trading with Hamburg in 1746-1747. NRS.E504.3.2]

LOCHORE, WILLIAM, a burgess of Kinghorn, husband of Isobel Boswall, a sasine, 1620. [NRS.RS31.II.356]

LOCHTY, JOHN, a seaman, husband of Isabel Moyes died 30 September 1785, parents of Thomas Lochty, born 1784, died 5 June 1814. [Aberdour gravestone]

LOCKHART, ROBERT, a fuller at Mill of Gaitmilk, husband of Katherine Steidmonthe, a sasine, 1632. [NRS.RS31.X.164]

LOGAN, HENRY, the younger, was admitted as a burgess of Crail in 1780. [CBR]

LOGAN, JOHN, in St Andrews, a sasine, 1645. [NRS.RS31.XV.121]

LOGIE, EUPHAN, in St Andrews, testament, 1711, Comm. St Andrews. [NRS]

LONIE, ALEXANDER, in St Andrews, in October 1798. [NRS.E326.15.31]

LOTHIAN, ALEXANDER, in St Andrews, was admitted as a burgess of St Andrews on 22 July 1760. [SABR]

LOTHIAN, ANDREW, a brewer in Cellardyke, Kilrenny, a Jacobite in 1745. [SHS.8.66/352]

LOTHIAN, HENRY, in Easter Fernie, husband of Isobel Bontaverone, a sasine, 1633. [NRS.RS31.X.206]

LOUDOUN, ROBERT, a sailor in Kirkcaldy, husband of Marjorie Anderson, a sasine, 1625. [NRS.RS31.VI.35]

LOUTFOUTE, ELIZABETH, spouse of James Lennox in Leuchars, a sasine, 1635. [NRS.RS31.XI.289]

LOVE, GAVIN, a butcher, son of William Love deacon of the butchers, was admitted as a burgess of Dunfermline on 24 September 1794. [DM]

LOVELL, WILLIAM, and his wife Janet Auchinleck, a sasine, 1649. [NRS.RS31.XXII.16]

LOW, DAVID, a sailor, husband of Betty Knox, born 1769, daughter of James Knox a merchant, died 8 March 1793. [Burntisland, St Columba's, gravestone]

LOW, DAVID, a farmer in Ballincreiff, was admitted as a burgess of St Andrews on 10 August 1769. [SABR]

LOW, JAMES, the elder, a mariner in Anstruther, a deed, 1715. [NRS.RD3.145.844]

LOW, JOHN, a skipper in St Andrews, was admitted as a burgess of St Andrews on 4 January 1771. [SABR]

LOWE, LACHLAN, in Burnside of Cupar, was admitted as a burgess of St Andrews on 9 November 1763. [SABR]

LOW, ROBERT, the younger, a merchant in St Monance, a deed, 1715. [NRS.RD3.145.19St Andrews. [NRS]

LOWRIE, JAMES, a fisherman in St Andrews, testament, 1711, Comm. St Andrews. [NRS]

LUCKLAW, MARGARET, wife of John Dairsie a skipper in Anstruther, a sasine, 1648. [NRS.RS31.XVI.239]

LUCKLAW, SIMON, of Wester Newton of Rires, husband of Isobel Ross, a sasine, 1654. [NRS.RS31.XIX.35]

LUGDOUN, ROBERT, a burgess of Anstruther, spouse of Janet Mitchell, a sasine, 1626. [NRS.RS31.VI.216]

LUMSDAINE, JOHN, a Major in the Service of the Honorable East India Company, a sasine, 1786. [NRS.RS31.1385]

LUMSDAINE, JOHN, son-in-law of David Kession, was admitted as a burgess of Dunfermline on 28 April 1797. [DM]

LUMSDEN, GEORGE, a skipper in Dysart, testament, 1752, Comm. St Andrews. [NRS]

LUMSDEN, GEORGE, a merchant in Falkland, a deed, 1788. [NRS.CS234.SEQNS.L.1.13]

LUMSDEN, Sir JAMES, of Innergellie, a Lieutenant Colonel in Germany in 1635. [NRS.RS31.XI.273]

LUMSDEN, JAMES, of Strathvithie, a deed, 1715. [NRS.RD3.146.584]

LUMSDEN, JAMES, a miller in Crichtonmill, was admitted as a burgess of Auchtermuchty on 16 July 1743. [ABR]

LUNDIE, JAMES, tacksman of the Inland Excise of Fife, 1689. [RPCS.XIV.73]

LUNDIE, JAMES, of Strathairly, a bailie of Kirkcaldy, a petition, 1689. [RPCS.XIV.147]

LUNDIE, JAMES, son of the late James Lundie of Clatto, parish of St Andrews, testament, 1708, Comm. St Andrews. [NRS]

LUNDIE, ROBERT, of Balgonie, a sasine, 1617. [NRS.RS31.I.10]

LUNDIE, THOMAS, master of the Robert and John of Anstruther trading with Bremen, Danzig, and Gothenburg, 1742-1744. [NRS.E504.3.1/2]

LUNDIN, MARY, wife of Thomas Adamson a Customs Officer in Leven, was served heir to her sister Margaret Lundin, daughter of Christopher Lundin a shipmaster there on 3 January 1751. [NRS.S/H]

LUNN, JOHN, son of Robert Lunn, a burgess of Crail and Admiral Depute of Fife, a sasine, 1654. [NRS.RS31.XIX.106]

LUTTIT, ISABEL, spouse of Andrew Birrell a burgess of Anstruther Easter, a sasine, 1638. [NRS.RS31.XII.115]

LYALL, ALEXANDER, a burgess of Newburgh by 1740. [NBR]

LYAL, ANDREW, a flax-dresser, son of Thomas Lyal a tailor burgess, was admitted as a burgess of Dunfermline on 18 July 1791. [DM]

LYALL, JOHN, schoolmaster of Anstruther, 1690. [SHS.4.2]

LYALL, PATRICK, a skipper in St Andrews, a deed, 1726. [NRS.B65.5.3/9]

LYALL, WILLIAM, a burgess of Pittenweem, spouse of Janet Rollie, a sasine, 1623. [NRS.RS31.V.121]

LYALL, WILLIAM, skipper of a drave boat of St Andrews, 1717. [NRS.B65.8.5.162]

LYNE, NELLY, in St Andrews in October 1798. [NRS.E326.15.31]

LYN, PATRICK, a sasine, 1649. [NRS.RS31.XVII.129]

LYN, STEPHEN, a sasine, 1649. [NRS.RS31.XVII.50]

MCARRAW, DAVID, a baker and brewer in Auchtermuchty, was served heir to the father David McArraw a meal-dealer there, on 9 October 1789. [NRS.S/H]

MCARRA, ROBERT, a watch-maker, son of James McArra a merchant burgess, was admitted as a burgess of Dunfermline on 2 May 1798. [DM]

M'CALL, NINIAN, in Wester Cleish, a sasine, 1627. [NRS.RS31.VII.124]

MCOLME, DAVID, an Excise officer in Cupar and St Andrews, ledger, 1699-1700. [NRS.CS238.MISC.23/4]

MCCORMICK, ALEXANDER, born 1741, died 17 February 1792. [Balmerino gravestone]

MCCORMICK, JOHN, late minister in St Andrews, testament, 1753, Comm. St Andrews. [NRS]

MCCORMICK, Reverend JOSEPH, born 1733, Principal of United Colleges of St Andrews, died 1799. [St Andrews gravestone]

MCCULLOCH, ALEXANDER, arch-beadle to the University of St Andrews, testament, 1745, Comm. St Andrews. [NRS]

MCDONALD, DANIEL, a meal-maker in St Andrews, was admitted as a burgess of St Andrews on 18 August 1758. [SABR]

MCDONALD, JAMES, in St Andrews, was admitted as a burgess of St Andrews on 31 January 1757. [SABR]

MCFADYEN, JOHN, a surgeon in Dunfermline, was admitted as a burgess and guilds-brother of Dunfermline on 4 June 1792. [DM]

MCFARLANE, DAVID, in St Andrews, was admitted as a burgess of St Andrews on 15 May 1755. [SABR]

MCFARRAN, CHARLES, died in April 1790. [St Andrews gravestone]

MCGILL, DAVID, of Nether Ranlkeillor, son of James McGill, spouse of Elizabeth Ruthven, a sasine, 1629. [NRS.RS31.VIII.27]

MAKGILL, HENRY, son of James MakGill of Rankeillour and his wife Jean Wemyss, graduated MA from St Andrews in 1615, minister at Dunfermline from 1622 to his death on 16 December 1642, husband of [1] Issobel Lindsay, [2] Margaret Wardlaw. [F.V.28]

MCGILL, JAMES, a mariner in St Monance, 1741, 1755. [NRS.B3.7.2;

MCGILL, JOHN, a merchant in Kirkcaldy, a deed, 1752. [NRS.RD4.178/2.376]

MCGULLAN, ROBERT, a burgess of Kinghorn, spouse of Catherine Wallange, a sasine 1631. [NRS.RS31.IX.307]

MACHAN, DAVID, born 1672, a merchant and a burgess of Culross, died on 8 April 1717. [Culross West gravestone]

MCHARDY, ANN, relict of Charles McHardy a vintner in Woodhaven, a deed, 1750. [NRS.RD3.210.468]

MCHARDIE, MARGARET, spouse of Robert Milne a tobacconist in Kennoway, a deed, 1749. [NRS.RD3.211/220]

MACKILROY, DAVID, [David Makili Roy?], from Culross, was admitted as a citizen of Posen in 1645. [Posen Burgess Register]

MCINTOSH, WILLIAM, a glazier in Easter Anstruther, a deed, 1715. [NRS.RD2.104.859]

MACK, DAVID, a merchant burgess of St Andrews, testament, 1712, Comm. St Andrews. [NRS]

MACKAY, HUGH, Major of the 2nd Battalion of Lord Sutherland's Regiment, was admitted as a burgess of St Andrews on 23 July 1761. [SABR]

MCKENZIE, JAMES, servant to Sir John Anstruther, was admitted as a burgess of St Andrews on 30 September 1765. [SABR]

MACKEY, WILLIAM, from Wodhaven, a mariner aboard HMS Tweed, died in Savanna, Georgia, probate, 1781, Prerogative Court of Canterbury. [TNA]

MACKIE, ANN, born 1753, died in June 1800, wife of John Anderson a wright in Dundee. [Forgan gravestone]

MACKIE, DAVID, born 1716, died 10 March 1793, husband of Christian Henderson, born 1728, died 20 May 1800. [Dunfermline Abbey gravestone]

MACKIE, GEORGE, master of the Industry of Kirkcaldy trading with Oporto in 1768. [NRS.E504.3.4]

MACKIE, JAMES, a skipper in Dunfermline, testament, 1787, Comm. St Andrews. [NRS]

MACKIE, JOHN, in Ceres, spouse of Agnes Oset, a sasine, 1626. [NRS.RS31.VI.40]

MACKIE, MARGARET, born 1793, naturalised in Charleston, South Carolina, in 1837. [NARA.M1183/1]

MACKIE, PATRICK, a smith, died in 1701. [Forgan gravestone]

MACKIE, THOMAS, eldest son of Thomas Mackie in Unstoun, Scoonie, a witness, 21 July 1654. [RGS.X.311]

MACKIE, THOMAS, in St Andrews, in October 1798. [NRS.E326.15.31]

MACKIESON, JOHN, town clerk of Crail, a sasine, 1617. [NRS.RS31.I.218]

MCKINLAY, DANIEL, master of the Concord of Dysart, bound for Quebec in 1811. [NRS.E504.15.92]

MACLACHLAN, PATRICK, a burgess of Newburgh by 1740. [NBR]

MACLAREN, JAMES, was admitted as a vintner burgess of Crail on 16 April 1801. [CBR]

MCLEAN, ALLAN, born 1750, son of Duncan MacLean in Cardross, minister at Dunfermline from 1791 until his death on 3 June 1836. [F.V.32]

MCLEOD, DAVID, from Fife, a member of the Scots Charitable Society of Boston, New England, in 1738. [NEHGS]

MCLEOD, NORMAND, of MacLeod, born 1707, died 21 July 1772. [St Andrews gravestone]

MACMILLAN, JAMES, from Dysart, to Konigsberg in 1589] [Records of the Burgh of Edinburgh, iv.543]

MCMILLAN, MALCOLM, schoolmaster of Inverkeithing, husband of Katherine Stewart, deed, 1685. [NRS.RD4.57.679]

MCNEISH, JOHN, born in Largo in 1785, a merchant, with his wife Janet and five children, emigrated from Falkirk to USA, naturalised in New York on 5 February 1828.

MCPHERSON, WILLIAM, in the Grange of Balmerino in 1717. [BA.634]

MCQUEEN, MARY, in Ferry-Port-on-Craig in 1762. [NRS.CH2.150.4.29]

MADEN, ANDREW, in Pilmuir, Forgan, testament, 1614, Comm. St Andrews. [NRS]

MAIDEN, ..., a surgeon in Crail, a Jacobite in 1745. [SHS.8.66/352]

MAIN, DAVID, son of Robert Main deacon of the shoemakers, was admitted as a burgess of Dunfermline on 27 March 1795. [DM]

MAIN, GEORGE, a soldier from St Andrews, married Margaret Brand from Aberdeen, in Geertruidenberg in the Netherlands, in 1638. [Geertruidenberg Marriage Register]

MAIN, HENRY, a tailor in East Wemyss, a sasine 1627. [NRS.RS31.VII.114]

MAINE, JAMES, a sailor in Aberdour, husband of Elizabeth Bryson in Newhaven, Rotterdam, testament, 23 February 1651, Amsterdam. [GAR.ONA.211.214.395]

MAIR, HENRY, a tailor in Newburgh, a sasine, 1620.
[NRS.RS31.II.153]

MAIR, WILLIAM, son of John Mair from London, was admitted as
a burgess and guilds-brother of Dunfermline on 15 September
1794. [DM]

MAKGILL, ROBERT, was served heir to his brother Patrcik Makgill,
second son of Sir James Makgill in Largo, on 28 February 1656.
[NRS.Retours.Fife.1449]

MALCOLM, ALEXANDER, master of the James of Kirkcaldy from
Dundee bound for New York with passengers in 1803.
[EA.4089][EEC.14230]

MALCOLM, CHARLES, a merchant in Kirkcaldy, a deed, 1715.
[NRS.RD4.117.291]

MALCOLM, GEORGE, a skipper in Kirkcaldy, testament, 1775,
Comm. St Andrews. [NRS]

MALCOLM, HENRY, in St Andrews, testament, 1709, Comm. St
Andrews. [NRS]

MALCOLM, JAMES, the younger of Balbeddie, a Jacobite in 1745.
[SHS.8.260/344]

MALCOLM, JAMES, from Kirkcaldy, a member of the Scots
Charitable Society of Boston, New England, in 1766. [NEHGS]

MALCOLM, JAMES, a weaver, son-in-law of John Ingles a mason
burgess, was admitted as a burgess of Dunfermline on 17 August
1795. [DM]

MALCOLM, JOHN, schoolmaster of Kirkcaldy, 1653. [DPD.I.358]

MALCOLM, JOHN, of Balbedie, was granted the lands and barony
of Inchegall alias Lochershyre, by Oliver Cromwell on 7 August
1654. [RGS.X.556]

MALCOLM, JOHN, a gardener in North Queensferry, a tack, 1733. [NRS.RH11.27.37/78]

MALLOCH, JOHN, a skipper in Kirkcaldy, aboard the Endeavour bound for Darien in 1698, testament, 1709, Comm. Edinburgh. [NRS]

MAN, ANDREW, from Dunfermline, emigrated via Glasgow to Pictou, Nova Scotia, aboard the Hector in 1773, settled in Noel, Nova Scotia.

MAN, JOHN, in Lochhead, and spouse Bessie Howie, a sasine, 1657. [NRS.RS31.XX.404]

MANDO, ROBERT, in St Monance, and spouse Isobel Elder, a sasine, 1617. [NRS.RS31.I.240]

MANSON, JOHN, salt-grieve to Lord Sinclair in Dysart, a deed, 1715. [NRS.RD3.145.705]

MANSON, JOHN, a vintner in Kirkcaldy, a deed, 1715. [NRS.RD3.146.530]

MAR, GEORGE, a boatman at Balmerino, testament, 1599. [NRS]

MARSHALL, JOHN, a merchant in Auchtermuchty, a deed, 1760. [NRS.B5.4.1/8]

MARSHALL, WILLIAM, in Leslie, and wife Margaret Anderson, a sasine, 1655. [NRS.RS31.XIX.226]

MARTIN, ALEXANDER, born 15 October 1761, son of Thomas Martin and his wife Elizabeth Bridges, a surgeon in the Royal Navy, died in July 1797. [Pittenweem gravestone]

MARTIN, DAVID, born 1576, graduated MA from St Andrews in 1595, minister at Auchtertool from 1605 until his death on 2 September 1636. [F.V.78]

MARTIN, GEORGE, of Claremont, St Andrews, testament, 1756, Comm. St Andrews. [NRS]

MARTIN, HELEN, in St Andrews, daughter of Reverend James Martin in Ballingray, testament, 1718, Comm. St Andrews. [NRS]

MARTIN, JAMES, a merchant in Pittenweem, was admitted as a burgess of St Andrews on 12 August 1755. [SABR]

MARTIN, JOHN, a rioter in Cupar, was banished to the American colonies in 1773. [NRS.B59.26.11.1.6.18][AJ.1322]

MARTIN, LUDOVIC, son of Stephen Marshall in La Rochelle, France, grandson of Isobel Auchenleck, a sasine, 1650. [NRS.RS31.XVII.318]

MARTIN, THOMAS, schoolmaster of Creich, 1690. [SHS.4.2]

MARTIN, THOMAS, a guilds-brother of St Andrews, testament, 1716, Comm. St Andrews. [NRS]

MARTIN, THOMAS, a merchant and bailie of Pittenweem, was admitted as a burgess of St Andrews on 1 August 1755. [SABR]

MASON, ANDREW, a butcher in St Andrews, a bond, 1706. [NRS.B65.5.2/2]

MASON, JOHN, a quartier in Burntisland, aboard the Unicorn bound for Darien in 1698, testament, 1707, Comm. Edinburgh. [NRS]

MASON, WILLIAM, born 1764, a merchant in Jamaica, died on 1 December 1841. [St Andrews gravestone]

MASSON, WILLAM, a skipper in St Andrews, son and heir of William Masson, 1748. [NRS.S/H]

MASSON, WILLIAM, born 1752, a butcher in St Andrews, died 1793, husband of Margaret Hay, born 1752, died 1834. [St Andrews gravestone]

MASTERTON, ALEXANDER, a bailie of Culross, was admitted as a burgess and guilds-brother of Dunfermline on 24 February 1804. [DM]

MASTERTON, JAMES, born 1749, a brewer in Culross, died in July 1791, husband of Emelia Arnot. [Culross Abbey gravestone]

MASTERTOUN, JOHN, died 5 June 1611. [Culross West gravestone]

MASTERTON, WILLIAM, a smith in Valleyfield, husband of Isabel Ballingall, born 1697, died 21 January 1752. [Culross gravestone]

MATHESON, ALEXANDER, from Anstruther, a member of the Scots Charitable Society of Boston, New England, in 1736. [NEHGS]

MATHEW, WILLIAM, a meal-maker in St Andrews, was admitted as a burgess of St Andrews on 2 February 1765. [SABR]

MATHISON, JAMES, a mason and feuar in Kilconquhar, and his wife Sophia, daughter of Andrew Briggs a merchant in Colinsburgh, a sasine, 1731. [NRS.GD62.325]

MATHIESON, ROBERT, in St Andrews, in October 1798. [NRS.E326.15.31]

MATTHEW, ALEXANDER, in Ferry-Port-on-Craig in 1782. [NRS.CH2.150.4.125]

MAURICE, WILLIAM, in St Andrews, in October 1798. [NRS.E326.15.31]

MAXWELL, JAMES, of Leckiebank, Auchtermuchtie, testament, 1718. [NRS.GD26.6.93]

MAXWELL, JAMES, born 1757, a dyer in St Andrews, died 7 March 1828, his wife Mary Paterson, born 1764, died 5 March 1839. [St Andrews gravestone]

MAXWELL, ROBERT, of Broombrae, born 1650, died 1724, husband of Margaret Bonthron, born 1653, died 1726. [Auchtermuchty gravestone]; son of Nicoll Maxwell, a deed, 1682. [NRS.GD26.4.929]

MAXWELL, WILLIAM, a merchant in Auchtermuchty, letters of horning, 1781. [NRS.GD26.4.1031]

MAYES, ALEXANDER, born in 1740, son of Philip Mayes and his wife Margaret Key, settled in Newark, Carriacou, near Grenada, died in Elie on 21 April 1791. [St Monance gravestone]

MEARNS, ROBERT, son of Robert Murray a skipper in Johnshaven, was apprenticed to George Barclay jr a skipper in Dysart for 3 years in 1780. [NRS.B21.5.2/378]

MEASSON, WILLIAM, late Convenor of the Trades of St Andrews, testament, 1739, Comm. St Andrews. [NRS]

MEIBLO, JAMES, a sailor in Dysart, aboard the St Andrew bound for Darien in 1698, testament, 1707, Comm. Edinburgh. [NRS]

MEIKLEJOHN, JAMES, from Dysart, died aboard HMS Royal William probate 1692, PCC. [TNA]

MELDRUM, DAVID, in Birchhill, Balmerino, in 1717. [BA.634]

MELDRUM, JOSHUA, MA, minister at Auchtertool from 1642 until 1651. [F.V.78]

MELDRUM, MARTIN, a weaver, son of William Meldrum a baker burgess, was admitted as a burgess of Dunfermline on 29 August 1791. [DM]

MELVILL, Master ALEXANDER, was served heir to his brother german John Melvill of Murdocairny on 25 August 1692. [NRS.Retours.Fife.1336]

MELVILL, ALAN, from Leven, son of Reverend Thomas Mevill in Scoonie, a merchant who settled in Boston, Massachusetts, in 1748, a member of the Scots Charitable Society of Boston in 1749, father of Thomas born 1751. [NEHGS][ANY.II.79]

MELVILLE, CHRISTIAN, wife of Professor Vilant in St Andrews, heir to her father John Melville, steward clerk there, on 5 February 1714. [NRS.S/H]

MELVILLE, DAVID, and his wife Janet Merton, parents of William Melville, born 1754, died September 1780. [Forgan gravestone]

MELVILLE, DAVID, a vintner in Ceres, was admitted as a burgess of St Andrews on 15 April 1762. [SABR]

MELVILLE, DAVID, of South Balmullo, was admitted as a burgess of St Andrews on 9 October 1770. [SABR]

MELVILLE, DAVID, farmer in Nether Strathkinness, first son of David Melville a burgess, was admitted as a burgess of St Andrews on 20 May 1771. [SABR]

MELVILLE, DAVID, of South Balmullo, was admitted as a burgess of St Andrews on 9 October 1770. [SABR]

MELVILLE, DAVID, born 1739, tenant in New Grange, died on 17 March 1787. [St Andrews gravestone]

MELVILLE, JAMES, farmer in Nether Strathkinness, second son of David Melville a burgess, was admitted as a burgess of St Andrews on 20 May 1771. [SABR]

MELVILLE, JOHN, a sailor in Kinghorn, aboard the Rising Sun bound for Darien in 1699, testament, 1707, Comm. Edinburgh. [NRS]

MELVILL, JOHN, from Leven, a member of the Scots Charitable Society of Boston, New England, in 1757. [NEHGS]

MELVILLE, JOHN, born 1794, husband of Willemina Durie, a shipmaster, died in St Vincent on 18 June 1834. [Pittenweem gravestone]

MELVILLE, MARGARET, relict of Patrick Mortimer a bailie of Cupar, papers, 1699-1703. [NRS.GD7.SEC1.59]

MELVILLE, THOMAS, in Boston, was admitted as a burgess of St Andrews on 13 September 1772. [SABR]

MELVILLE, WILLIAM, master of the Kirkcaldy Packet of Pittenweem trading with St Sebastian in Spain in 1731. [NRS.CE52.4.1]

MELVILLE, WILLIAM, was admitted as a shoemaker burgess of Crail on 2 October 1799. [CBR]

MELVILLE, Major, of Cairny, was admitted as a burgess of St Andrews on 2 June 1766. [SABR]

MELVIN, JAMES, from Pittenweem, a member of the Scots Charitable Society of Boston, New England, in 1730. [NEHGS]

MENZIES, ALEXANDER, a dyker in St Andrews, was admitted as a burgess of St Andrews on 7 January 1758. [SABR]

MENZIES, ROBERT, son of Alexander Menzies a guilds-brother, was admitted as a burgess of St Andrews on 6 March 1766. [SABR]

MERCER, JAMES, a shoemaker in Kincardine, son-in-law of William Kellock a tailor burgess, was admitted as a burgess of Dunfermline on 20 January 170-. [DM]

MERCER, DAVID, formerly a mason in St Andrews, later in Perth, testament, 1714, Comm. St Andrews. [NRS]

MERCHISTON, ROBERT, a surgeon's mate from Fife, aboard the St Andrew bound for Darien in 1698, testament, 1707, Comm. Edinburgh. [NRS]

METHVEN, ALEXANDER, son of Thomas Methven and his wife Margaret Symers, a surgeon, died 1807 in South Carolina. [St Andrews gravestone]

METHVEN, GEORGE, portioner of Byrehills, St Andrews, testament, 1700, Comm. St Andrews. [NRS]

METHVEN, JOHN, third son of Thomas Methven a burgess of St Andrews, was admitted as a burgess of St Andrews on 22 December 1769. [SABR]

MICHAELSON, JOHN, graduated MA from St Andrews in 1583, minister at Burntisland from 1616 until 1640. [F.V.81]

MIGGLESTON, THOMAS, a sailor in Inverkeithing, husband of Janet Ferguson, aboard the Rising Sun bound for Darien in 1699, testament, 1707, Comm. Edinburgh. [NRS]

MILL, CHARLES, son of Thomas Mill of Blair and his wife Janet Young, a Lieutenant Colonel of the 55th Regiment of Foot, died on 20 February 1780 in Coorg, India. [Crombie gravestone]

MILL, PATRICK, a fisherman in St Andrews, was admitted as a burgess of St Andrews on 26 July 1759. [SABR]

MILLER, ALEXANDER, sometime Deacon of the Butchers in St Andrews, testament, 1713, Comm. St Andrews. [NRS]

MILLER, ALEXANDER, a shoemaker in St Andrews, was admitted as a burgess of St Andrews on 12 August 1774. [SABR]

MILLAR, DAVID, servant to Magnus Aytoun, clerk of Burntisland, 1654. [RGS.X.311]

MILLER, DAVID, a sailor in Kirkcaldy, aboard the Dolphin bound for Darien in 1698, testament, 1707, Comm. Edinburgh. [NRS]

MILLER, DAVID, second son of David Miller a burgess of St Andrews, was admitted as a burgess of St Andrews on 1 September 1773. [SABR]

MILLER, JAMES, a Covenanter from Kirkcaldy, transported aboard the St Michael of Scarborough to the West Indies in 1678. [RPCS.VI.76]

MILLER, JAMES, a fisherman in St Andrews, 1717. [NRS.B65.8.5.162]

MILLER, JOHN, a sailor from Auchtertool, son of John Miller, aboard the Dolphin bound for Darien in 1698, testament, 1707, Comm. Edinburgh. [NRS]

MILLAR, JOHN, master of the Mercury of Kirkcaldy from Kirkcaldy to New York with passengers in 1799. [EA.3658/3711]; testament, 1809, Comm. St Andrews. [NRS]

MILLER, ROBERT, tenant in Craigmiln, Lindores, a bond, 1800. [NRS.CS271.441]

MILLER, THOMAS, a mariner in Kinghorn, testament, 1710, Comm. Edinburgh. [NRS]

MILLER, THOMAS, a meal-maker in St Andrews, a bond, 1706. [NRS.B65.5.2/3]

MILLER, WILLIAM, of Mugdrum, a deed, 1715. [NRS.RD4.117.596]

MILLER, WILLIAM, master of the Peter and Betty of Newburgh trading with Christiansand in Norway in 1758. [NRS.E504.27.4]

MILLS, JOHN, master of the Peter and Rachel of Limekilns trading with Rotterdam in 1745. [NRS.E504.27.1]

MILNE, JAMES, a skipper in Newburgh, testament, 1803, Comm. St Andrews. [NRS]

MILNE, ROBERT, a skipper in St Andrews, a deed, 1726. [NRS.B65.5.3/9]

MITCHELL, ALEXANDER, born 1761, a shoemaker, died 1829. [St Andrews gravestone]

MITCHELL, ALEXANDER, son of Walter Mitchell in Coul, Markinch, apprenticed to Andrew Sterling a shipbuilder in Dysart for 4 years, in 1790. [NRS.B21.5.3/249]

MITCHELL, ALEXANDER, born 1799, son of George Mitchell and his wife Elizabeth Chiene, a Lieutenant of the Madras Native Infantry, died at sea on 31 March 1827. [St Andrews gravestone]

MITCHELL, BRUCE, in the Service of the Honorable East India Company, was admitted as a burgess of Dunfermline on 5 Jun 1797. [DM]

MITCHELL, CHARLES, from Burntisland, a seaman aboard the Princess, probate 1690, PCC. [TNA]

MITCHELL, CHARLES, a skipper in Wester Wemyss, a deed, 1715. [NRS.RD2.104.869]

MITCHELL, DAVID, schoolmaster of Anstruther Wester, a sasine, 1634. [NRS.RS30.11.50]

MITCHELL, DAVID, a merchant in Kirkcaldy, deeds, 1715. [NRS.RD3.145.621-637; RD4.117.635]

MITCHELL, DAVID, a maltman in St Andrews, and his spouse Janet Fairfoull, a deed, 1715. [NRS.B65.5.3/218]; testament, 1735, Comm. St Andrews. [NRS]

MITCHEL, HENDRY, born 1662, died 18 October 1724, husband of Katherine Wilson, born 1663, died 2 September 1742. [Balmerino gravestone]

MITCHELL, JANET, relict of William Bell a weaver in St Andrews, testament, 1797, Comm. St Andrews. [NRS]

MITCHELL, MATHEW, graduated MA from Edinburgh University in 1739, minister at Auchterderran from 1741 until his death on 23 March 1782. [F.V.77]

MITCHELL, THOMAS, a soldier from Cupar, married Iffijen Kry in Haarlem, the Netherlands, in 1597. [Haarlem Marriage Register]

MITCHELL, THOMAS, a weaver in St Andrews, was admitted as a burgess of St Andrews on 2 January 1771. [SABR]

MITCHELL, WILLIAM, in Balrymonth, a bond, 1706. [NRS.B65.5.2/28]

MITCHELL, WILLIAM, born 1742 in Fife, emigrated aboard the Clementina to Philadelphia in 1775. [TNA.T47.12]

MITCHELSON, MATHEW, master of the Ann of Kirkcaldy trading with Norway in 1749. [NRS.E504.3.2]

MITCHELLSON, WILLIAM, a councillor of Burntisland in 1689. [RPCS.XIV.455]

MOFFAT, DAVID, a mariner from Leven, died overseas aboard the Formosa, probate 1680, Prerogative Court of Canterbury. [TNA]

MOIR, HENRY, born in Linlithgow, minister at Auchtertool from 1746 until his death on 18 June 1786. [F.V.79]

MOIR, JAMES, a minister from Auchintool, emigrated to America in 1739, died on 31 December 1766 in Edgecombe County, North Carolina. [SM.28.615][NRS.CS16.1.134][SPG.3.20]

MOIR, JAMES, son of David Moir a weaver burgess, was admitted as a burgess of Dunfermline on 11 September 1802. [DM]

MOIR, JOHN, schoolmaster of Wemyss, 1690. [SHS.4.2]

MONCREIFF, ELIZABETH, spouse of Thomas Brown in France, formerly in Crail, a deed, 1672. [NRS.RD4.31.320]

MONCREIFF, GEORGE, of Sachope, bailie of Crail, a bond, 15 July 1691. [NRS.PC12.16.100]

MONCREIFF, Colonel GEORGE, born 1709, died in November 1771, his wife Helen Skene, born 1719, died in March 1816. [Auchtermuchty gravestone]

MONCREIFF, JAMES, of Sauchop, was admitted as a burgess of St Andrews on 27 February 1758. [SABR]

MONCREIFF, KATHERINE, relict of John Balfour Hay of Leys and Randerston, died 26 January 1805. [Auchtermuchty gravestone]

MONCREIFF, PATRICK, of Myres and Reedie, a Member of Parliament for Fife, died in 1709. [Auchtermuchty gravestone]

MONCREIFF, PATRICK, born 1751, died 1790, his wife Lucy Hay, died in November 1822. [Auchtermuchty gravestone]

MONCREIFF, WILLIAM, a shipmaster in Burntisland, deeds, 1685-1686, [NRS.RD3.66.537; RD4.58.302]

MONCREIFF, WILLIAM, a deed, 1707; late Dean of Guild of St Andrews, spouse Janet Lowrie, testaments, 1715, 1723, Comm. St Andrews. [NRS.RD2.94.984]

MONRO, ALEXANDER, Provost of St Salvador's College in St Andrews, testaments, 1709/1714, Comm. St Andrews. [NRS]

MONYPENNY, ALEXANDER, of Pitmillie, a deed, 1715. [NRS.RD3.145.736]

MONYPENNY, Colonel ALEXANDER, of Pitmilly, versus Robert Donaldson, a shipmaster in New York, then in St Andrews, 1765. [NRS.CS16.1.122]

MOODIE, JAMES, son of John Moodie of Cocklaw a burgess, was admitted as a burgess of Dunfermline on 8 February 1810. [DM]

MOODIE, THOMAS, from Cocklaw, Beith, husband of Ann McKenzie, settled in Georgia in 1750, Secretary to the Governor. [Houstouns of Georgia, page 134]; a land grant in Savannah on 6 October 1767. [Georgia Grant book F.386]

MORAY, JOHN, fourth son of Robert Moray of Abercairny, was educated at Edinburgh University, graduated MA in 1595, minister at Dunfermline from 1620 to 1622, died in Prestonpans in 1632. Husband of [1] Margaret Leslie, [2] Mary Melville. [F.V..28]

MORE, DAVID, master of the Expedition of Cellardyke trading with Danzig in 1743. [NRS.E504.3.1]

MORES, CHRISTIAN, relict of Thomas Shoolbred a baker in Auchtermuchty, a deed, 1757. [NRS.B5.4.1/1]

MORGAN, CHRISTIAN, from Dunfermline, married Allan Maclean from Mull, in the Scots Kirk in Rotterdam on 16 January 1709. [GAR]

MORGAN, JOHN, a sailor in Leven, aboard the St Andrew bound for Darien in 1698, testament, 1707, Comm. Edinburgh. [NRS]

MORISEITE, JOHN, a sailor in Burntisland, husband of Margaret Gray, aboard the Unicorn bound for Darien in 1698, testament, 1707, Comm. Edinburgh. [NRS]

MORRICE, ALEXANDER, a waulker in Cupar, was admitted as a burgess of St Andrews in 1774. [SABR]

MORRICE, CHARLES, son of Michael Morrice a burgess of St Andrews, was admitted as a burgess of St Andrews on 31 January 1757. [SABR]

MORRICE, DAVID, of Allanhill, was admitted as a burgess of St Andrews on 4 June 1761, [SABR]; MORRIS, DAVID, of Allanhill, born 1740, died 25 December 1811, husband of Margaret Bonthrone, born 1751, died 1 July 1802. [St Andrews gravestone]

MORRICE, JOHN, first son of John Morrice a weaver in St Andrews, was admitted as a burgess of St Andrews on 24 January 1772. [SABR]

MORRICE, JOHN, of Allanhill, was admitted as a burgess of St Andrews on 18 April 1757. [SABR]

MORRICE, JOHN, in St Andrews, was admitted as a burgess of St Andrews on 11 December 1757. [SABR]

MORRIS, DAVID, born in 1793, son of William Morris and his wife Elizabeth Simpson, died on 18 May 1818 in Dominica. [Kemback gravestone]

121

MORRISON, HENRY, a smith in Inverkeithing, son-in-law of Thomas Gibson a wright in Dunfermline, was admitted as a burgess of Dunfermline on 5 September 1796. [DM]

MORRISON, JAMES, of Naughton, was admitted as a burgess of St Andrews on 11 September 1761. [SABR]

MORRISON, JOHN, born 1781 in Fife, a merchant who was naturalised in Charleston, South Carolina, in 1807. [NARA.M1183/1]

MORRISON, NICOL, a tiler in Dysart, husband of Christina Clark, sasine, 1622. [NRS.RS31.IV.42]

MORRISON, SIMON, born 1796, a cabinet-maker, was naturalised in Charleston, South Carolina, in 1830. [NARA.M1183/1]

MORRISON, THOMAS, from West Wemyss, settled in Leyden, Holland, before 1636. [NRS.S/H.1636]; sasines, 1631, 1637. [NRS.RS31.IX.190; XI.369]

MORTIMER, JOHN, a bailie of Dysart, a deed, 1715. [NRS.RD2.104.573]

MORTIMER, PATRICK, a merchant in Cupar, husband of Margaret Melvill, sasine, 1659. [NRS.RS31.XXII.80]

MORTON, ARTHUR, a burgess of Crail, husband of Cecil Ross, a sasine, 1648. [NRS.RS31.XVI.285]

MORTON, THOMAS CAMPBELL, born 1772 in Fife, a merchant in New York from 1793, died there on 30 April 1833. [ANY.I.341]

MORTON, WALTER, master of the Antelope of Burntisland trading with Konigsberg, Danzig, Elsinore, Norway, Bruges, Flanders, Fecamp, Dieppe, Honfleur, Rouen, St Martins, Rochelle,

Bordeaux, Lisbon, Spain, Plymouth, Dover, London, and Yarmouth, 1589-1600. [NRS.RH9.1.5]

MOTION, GEORGE, born 1761, late Deacon of the Shoemakers, died 16 May 1801, husband of Magdalene Bell, born 1753, died 2 June 1818. [St Andrews gravestone]

MOUBRAY, JAMES, and his wife Margaret Kinninmond, a bond, 1710. [RGS.RH11.27.32/49]

MOUBRAY, JOHN, of Cockairney, born 1603, died 9 November 1665. [Dalgetty gravestone]

MOULTRIE, JOHN, born 1702, son of John Moultrie and his wife Catharine Craik in Culross, educated at Edinburgh University, settled in Charleston, South Carolina, in 1729, died 1771. [SCHGM.5.242]

MOULTRIE, WALTER, a sailor in Markinch, son of George Moultrie, aboard the Union bound for Darien in 1698, died there, testament, 1707, Comm. Edinburgh. [NRS]

MOYES, JAMES, a seaman in Kinghorn, a deed, 1680. [NRS.RD3.48.130]

MOYES, JAMES, a cooper in Kinghorn, husband of Janet Spowart, aboard the Dolphin bound for Darien in 1698, testament, 1707, Comm. Edinburgh. [NRS]

MOYES, JAMES, a writer in Kirkcaldy, a deed, 1715. [NRS.RD4.116.930]

MOYES, MATHEW, a tenant in Pitcorthie, a deed, 1715. [NRS.RD4.116.199]

MOYES, WILLIAM, a cooper in Burntisland, aboard the Dolphin bound for Darien in 1698. [NRS.GD406.C23.5]; testament, 1707, Comm. Edinburgh. [NRS]

MUCKERSIE, GEORGE, a maltman in Wester Wemyss, a deed, 1715. [NRS.RD3.144.155]

MUDIE, JAMES, a midshipman aboard HMS Warrior, son of John Mudie of Muirhead, a sasine 1783. [NRS.RS.Fife.681]

MUIR, ALEXANDER, a sailor from Auchtermuchty, aboard the Rising Sun bound for Darien in 1699, testament, 1707, Comm. Edinburgh. [NRS]

MUIR, JAMES, the Deacon of the Smiths of St Andrews, was admitted as a burgess of St Andrews on 26 February 1763. [SABR]

MUIRHEAD, THOMAS, from Linktown of Abbotshall, a merchant in Rotterdam in the Netherlands, a deed in 1688. [NRS.RD4.62.816]

MUNRO, CATHERINE, born 1778 in Fife, daughter of Robert and Margaret Munro, settled in Charleston, South Carolina, before 1807, naturalised there in 1828. [NARA.M1183/1][Crail gravestone]

MUNRO, JAMES, a mariner from Fife, was naturalised in Charleston, South Carolina, in 1796. [NARA.M1183/1]

MURE, ALEXANDER, master of the Catto of Burntisland trading with Bruges, Flanders, in 1670. [NRS.E72.9.4]

MURE, JAMES, a merchant burgess of Kirkcaldy, and his spouse Jeanet Hepburne, a joint grant of the lands and barony of Alloa, by Oliver Cromwell on 21 July 1654. [RGS.X.312]

MURIE, DAVID, master of the Jane of Limekilns trading with Scandinavia in 1749. [NRS.E504.3.2]

MURIESON, Reverend JAMES, Principal of New College of St Andrews, died 30 July 1779, [St Andrews gravestone]; testament,

1779, Comm. St Andrews. [NRS]; spouse Annabella Trent, died 22 November 1761. [St Andrews gravestone]

MURRAY, ALEXANDER, born 1797, son of Andrew Murray and his wife Janet Mackie, died 1821 in Jamaica. [Auchterderran gravestone][F.5.77]

MURRAY, ANDREW, born 1749, son of Reverend Alexander Murray, graduated MA from King's College, Aberdeen, in 1774, minister at Auchterderran from 1783 until his death on 29 April 1844. [F.V.77]

MURRAY, ANTHONY, of Grante, Culross, a Jacobite in 1745. [SHS.8.148/338]

MURRAY, GEORGE, schoolmaster of St Andrews, relict Margaret Inglis, testament, 24 April 1685, Comm. St Andrews. [NRS]

MURRAY, JOHN, a meal-maker in St Andrews, was admitted as a burgess of St Andrews on 21 December 1762. [SABR]

MURRAY, Sir WILLIAM, of Blebo, a contract, November 1638. [NRS.GD7.SEC1.43]

MURRAY, WILLIAM, the younger, a councillor of Burntisland in 1689. [RPCS.XIV.455]

MUSTARD, JAMES, born 1719, died 6 February 1763. [Culross Abbey gravestone]

MUTER, WILLIAM, of Annfield, born 1732, died 12 June 1816. [Crombie gravestone]

MYLES, DAVID, master of the Peter and Betty of Newburgh trading with Rotterdam, Danzig, Gothenburg and Copenhagen, 1755 to 1757. [NRS.E504.27.4]

NAIRNE, ALEXANDER, bailie of St Andrews, testament, 1707, Comm. St Andrews. [NRS]

NAIRN, ALEXANDER, of Saintford, a deed, 1715. [NRS.RD2.104.433]

NAIRNE, GEORGE, minister at Burntisland from 1649 until 1662, died in June 1670. [F.V.81]

NAIRN, JAMES, master of the Margaret of Elie trading between Kirkcaldy and Bruges, Flanders, in 1682. [NRS.E72.9.12]

NAIRN, JAMES, master of the Margaret of Elie trading with Gothenburg in 1739. [NRS.CE52.4.1]

NAIRNE, Colonel JOHN, Provost of St Andrews, testament, 1790, Comm. St Andrews. [NRS]

NAIRN, Sir WILLIAM, of Dunino, was admitted as a burgess of St Andrews on 2 February 1761. [SABR]

NEAVE, ALEXANDER, servant to Bethune of Blebo, was admitted as a burgess of St Andrews on 1 September 1761. [SABR]

NEISH, ELSPETH, spouse of Andrew Thomason the younger Deacon of the Shoemakers of St Andrews, testament, 1713, Comm. St Andrews. [NRS]

NEISH, HENRY, born 1688, a mason in St Andrews, died on 22 June 1781. [St Andrews gravestone]

NEISH, THOMAS, a wright in St Andrews, testament, 1713, Comm. St Andrews. [NRS]

NESS, GEORGE, was admitted as a weaver burgess of Cupar on 18 December 1760. [CBR]

NICOLL, BENJAMIN, servant to Provost Dempster, was admitted as a burgess of St Andrews on 30 September 1765. [SABR]

NICOLL, FRANCIS, MA, minister at Auchtertool from 1787 until 1797. [F.V.79]

NICOLSON, HENRY, in St Andrews, heir to his father Henry Nicolson a burgess and guilds-brother there who died in January 1758. [NRS.S/H]; was admitted as a burgess of St Andrews on 20 September 1758. [SABR]

NICHOLSON, JOHN, born 1711, from Anstruther, emigrated to Jamaica in July 1729. [CLRO/AIA]

NICHOLSON, WILLIAM, born 1748, died in Macao, China, in 1801. [Burntisland, St Columba's, gravestone]

NISBET, JAMES, a meal-maker in St Andrews, was admitted as a burgess of St Andrews on 28 December 1757. [SABR]

NISBET, JAMES, of Letham, born 1737, died on 4 October 1780 in Jamaica. [Nisbet of that Ilk, p.108, London, 1941]

NISBET, JAMES, the elder, a wheel-wright in St Andrews, husband of Margaret Thomson, parents of Thomas Nisbet a baker in St Andrews, a deed, 1791. [NRS.B65.6.7/81]

NIVEN, JOHN, a cooper in Leven, husband of Elizabeth Durie, a sasine, 1654. [NRS.RS31.XIX.104]

NIVEN, ROBERT, a meal-maker in St Andrews, was admitted as a burgess of St Andrews on 25 March 1758. [SABR]

NORIE, ROBERT, MA, minister at Dunfermline in 1676. [F.V.29]

NORMAND, ALEXANDER, in St Andrews in October 1798. [NRS.E326.15.31]

NORMAND, JAMES, master of the Peggy of Kirkcaldy trading with North Carolina in 1772. [NRS.E504.20.8]

NORMAND, JOHN, a burgess of Strathmiglo, husband of Margaret Bickerton, a sasine, 1651. [NRS.RS31.XVIII.100]

NORMAND, MARGARET, daughter of John Normand in Leuchars, a sasine, 1637. [NRS.RS31.XII.87]

NORMAND, MATTHEW, master of the Christian of Dysart trading with Riga in 1767. [NRS.E504.27.4]

NORMAND, WILLIAM, a burgess of Strathmiglo, husband of Margaret Thomson, a sasine, 1624. [NRS.RS31.V.320]

NORMAND, WILLIAM, only son of the late William Normand, a carpenter burgess of Dysart, a deed, 1776. [NRS.B21.5.2/257]

NORRIE, ANDREW, a burgess of Cupar, husband of Isobel Mitchell, a sasine, 1618. [NRS.RS31.I.279]

NORRIE, JOHN, a burgess of Anstruther, spouse Agnes Dason, a sasine, 1619. [NRS.RS31.II.148]

NORRY, LAWRENCE, a tailor, son of David Norry tailor burgess of St Andrews, was admitted as a burgess of St Andrews on 10 January 1758. [SABR]

NORVELL, ISOBEL, spouse of George Moncrieff of Reidie, a sasine, 1619. [NRS.RS31.II.156]

OGG, HENDRIE, a watch-maker in Dunfermline, was admitted as a burgess of Dunfermline on 8 December 1809. [DM]

OGILVIE, GILBERT, an excise Officer in Ceres, was admitted as a burgess of St Andrews on 29 November 1755. [SABR]

OGILVIE, GUSTAVUS, a journeyman shoemaker in St Andrews, was admitted as a burgess of St Andrews on 28 November 1771. [SABR]

OGILVIE, JOSEPH, a councillor of Auchtermuchty, 1784. [NRS.CS228.A5.23]

OGILVIE, PHILIP, a councillor of Auchtermuchty, 1784. [NRS.CS228.A5.23]

OLIPHANT, ANDREW, a tenant in Scoonyhill, St Andrews, testaments, 1785-1786, Comm. St Andrews. [NRS]

OLIPHANT, CALVIN, a seaman in Burntisland, bound for Port Nelson on Hudson Bay in 1683. [HBRS.9.90]

OLIPHANT, JOHN, a foremast-man in Kirkcaldy, son of James Oliphant and his wife Isobel Wyse, aboard the Caledonia bound for Darien in 1698, testament, 1707, Comm. Edinburgh. [NRS]

OLIPHANT, JOHN, of Carpow, a deed, 1715. [NRS.RD3.144.72]

OLIPHANT, JOHN, a burgess of Newburgh by 1740. [NBR]

OLIPHANT, JOHN, late treasurer of Crail, was admitted as a burgess of St Andrews on 27 February 1758. [SABR]

OLIPHANT, JOHN, servant to George Lindesy of Wormiston, was admitted as a burgess of St Andrews on 14 March 1759. [SABR]

OLIPHANT, LAURENCE, a sailor in Williamstown, aboard the Caledonia bound for Darien in 1698, testament, 1708, Comm. Edinburgh. [NRS]

ORME, GEORGE, in Newburgh, 1657. [RGS.X.622]

ORROCK, ALEXANDER, of that Ilk, a sasine 1646. [NRS.RS31.XV.416]

ORROCK, ALEXANDER, a sailor from Fife, husband of Rachel Simpson, aboard the St Andrew bound for Darien in 1698, testament, 1707, Comm. Edinburgh. [NRS]

ORROCK, HENRY, portioner of Over Grange of Kinghorn Wester, a sasine, 1633. [NRS.RS31.X.181

ORROCK, JAMES, a shoemaker in Kinghorn, a deed, 1752. [NRS.RD2.172.283]

ORROK, JOHN, from Burntisland, was admitted as a citizen of Posen, Poland, in 1645. [Posen Burgess Roll]

ORROCK, JOHN, a sailor in Kinghorn, husband of Isobel Steedman, to Darien in 1698, testament, 1707, Comm. Edinburgh. [NRS]

ORROK, ROBERT, portioner of Overgrange, Aberdour, a deed, 1635. [NRS.B9.14.32]

ORROK, THOMAS, master of the Isobel and Jean of Aberdour trading with Norway in 1730-1731. [NRS.CE52.1.3]

ORROCK, WALTER, a merchant in Leven, a deed, 1752. [NRS.RD2.171.400]; a merchant in Methil versus Alexander Gordon, a merchant in Boston, New England, 1754. [NRS.AC7.46.101-106]

OSSET, PATRICK, servant to Patrick Kyninmonth of that Ilk, a sasine, 1637. [NRS.RS31.XII.47]

OSWALD, HENDRY, a bailie of Kirkcaldy, a petition, 1689. [RPCS.XIV.147]

OSWALD, HENDRY, born 1658, tenant of Geld's Mill, died 29 June 1721, father of John Oswald tenant in Cragkeely. [Burntisland, Kirkton, gravestone]

OSWALD, HENRY, son of Thomas Oswald in Kirkcaldy, probate 1726, Essex County, Virginia.

OSWALD, JAMES, of Dunnikier, a deed of factory, 1724. [NRS.RH11.27.33/294]

OSWALD, JAMES TOWNSEND, of Dunnikier, was admitted as a burgess of St Andrews on was admitted as a burgess of St Andrews on 21 September 1765. [SABR]

OSWALD, JOHN, a writer in Kirkcaldy, a deed of factory, 1723. [NRS.RH11.27.33/249]

OSWALD, ROBERT C. B., born in 1784, son of J. T. Oswald of Dunnikier, a Lieutenant Colonel of the Greek Light Infantry, died in 1848. [Kirkcaldy gravestone]

OUCHTERLONY, JAMES, in St Andrews, was admitted as a burgess of St Andrews on 21 January 1755. [SABR]

OVERTON, WILLIAM, a cabinet-maker in St Andrews, a contract of co-partnery in 1791. [NRS.B65.5.7/66]

OVERTON, Mrs, in St Andrews in October 1798. [NRS.E326.15.31]

PAGE, DAVID, a merchant in Cupar, a sasine, 1617. [NRS.RS31.I.91]

PAGE, HARRY, schoolmaster of Kilrenny, a sasine, 1659. [NRS.RS30.22.112]

PAGE, JAMES, a burgess of Strathmiglo, a sasine, 1659. [NRS.RS31.XXII.44]

PALMER, THOMAS, a sasine, 1618. [NRS.RS31.I.272]

PARK, ALEXANDER, Captain in the Honorable East Company Service, a sasine in 1786. [NRS.RS31.1464]

PARK, JAMES, from Dysart, a seaman aboard the Zeeland warship Swanenburg in 1664-1665. [Zeeuws Archief, Rekenkamer C6984]

PARK, JOHN, from Dysart, a seaman aboard the Zeeland warship Swanenburg in 1664-1665. [Zeeuws Archief, Rekenkamer C6984]

PARKER, MATTHEW, a watch-maker, son of John Parker a smith burgess, was admitted as a burgess of Dunfermline on 8 February 1788. [DM]

PARKIE, JAMES, a burgess of Crail, a sasine, 1623. [NRS.RS31.V.204]

PARROK, HENRY, a tailor in Linktoun of Abbotshall, husband of Margaret Stocks, a sasine, 1649. [NRS.RS31.XVII.88A]

PATERSON, ALEXANDER, third son of Andrew Paterson a baker in St Andrews, was admitted as a burgess of St Andrews on 15 December 1757. [SABR]

PATERSON, CHARLES, master of the Bess of Ferry-Port-on-Craig trading with Rotterdam in 1722-1723. [NRS.CE.1.3]

PATERSON, JAMES, eldest son of Andrew Paterson a baker in St Andrews, was admitted as a burgess of St Andrews on 15 December 1768. [SABR]

PATTERSON, JAMES, MD, a physician in Dundee, was admitted as a burgess of St Andrews on 3 November 1768. [SABR]

PATERSON, MARGARET, daughter of John Paterson a surgeon apothecary in Newburgh, and spouse of William Laing a wright there, a deed, 1752. [NRS.RD3.211/2.581]

PATERSON, ROBERT, a merchant in Dunfermline, a deed, 1715. [NRS.RD3.145.728]

PATERSON, ROBERT, a merchant in Dunfermline, and Susana Henderson, daughter of James Henderson, a marriage contract, 1722. [NRS.B20.6.4/108]

PATERSON, ROBERT, in St Andrews, was admitted as a burgess of St Andrews on 17 December 1771. [SABR]

PATERSON, ROBERT, son of the late Andrew Paterson the Deacon of the Bakers of St Andrews, was admitted as a burgess of St Andrews on 4 March 1758. [SABR]

132

PATERSON, ROBERT, born 1779, son of Robert Paterson and his wife Rosetta Maitland, died 23 July 1803 on Great Courland Estate, Tobago. [St Andrews gravestone]

PATERSON, WILLIAM, from Kirkcaldy, settled in Bergen, Norway, by 1627. [NRS.S/H.1627]; sasines, 1626. [NRS.RS31.258/290]

PATERSON, WILLIAM, born 1729, a shoemaker, died 24 September 1798, husband of Agnes Anderson. [St Andrews gravestone]

PATTIE, ROBERT, in St Andrews in October 1798. [NRS.E326.15.31]

PATTON, ALEXANDER, born 13 December 1779 in Auchtermuchty, a cooper who settled in New York on 22 June 1801. [SG.32.3]

PATON, ALEXANDER, born 26 November 1786, a surgeon in Bombay, died 26 April 1852. [Torryburn gravestone]

PATON, ANDREW, a mason and quarrier in Leuchars, a contract, 1751. [NRS.RD3.211/2.144]

PATON, JAMES, born 1682, son of James Paton of Balilisk, died 2 November 1729. [Crombie gravestone]

PATON, JOHN, master of the Friendship of Pittenweem trading with Norway and Danzig in 1743-1752. [NRS.E504.3.1.2]

PATON, WILLIAM, of Lochhead, graduated MA from St Andrews in 1585, minister at Aberdour, Beath, and Dalgetty, 1611, died in 1634, husband of Jean Balcanqual, parents of James, John, William, Margaret, and Jean. [F.V.2]

PATRICK, AGNES, wife of David Thompson a tailor in Buckhaven, a sasine, 1627. [NRS.RS31.VII.162]

PATRICK, ANDREW, a smith in the Fluirs of Buckhaven, husband of Christina Thomson, sasine, 1623. [NRS.RS31.IV.316]

PATULLO, GEORGE, of Balhousie, was served heir to his father Master George Patullo of St Salvador's College, University of St Andrews, on 6 April 1686. [NRS.Retours. Fife.1259]

PATTULLO, NATHANIEL, master of the Cambridge of Elie trading with Cadiz in 1750. [NRS.E504.3.3]

PAULL, GRISELL, wife of Florence Smyth in Anstruther, a sasine, 1618. [NRS.RS31.I.257]

PAUL, JOHN, a slater from Kelty, was admitted as a burgess of Dunfermline on 3 June 1788. [DM]

PEACOCK, ADAM, tenant in Roscobie, husband of Elspeth Bowman, a tack, 1711. [NRS.RH11.27.32/110]

PEACOCK, JAMES, a burgess of Kilrenny, a sasine, 1636. [NRS.RS31.XI.332]

PEARSON, ANDREW, a maltman burgess of Dunfermline, a bond, 1697. [NRS.B20.6.3]

PEARSON, CHRISTINA, spouse of Alexander Matheson in Kilconquhar, a sasine, 1624. [NRS.RS31.V.194]

PEARSON, DAVID, in Kirkton of Abbotshall, a sasine, 1640. [NRS.RS31.XIII.37]

PEARSON, ELSPETH, a rioter in Cupar, was transported to America in 1773. [NRS.B59.26.1.6.18][AJ.1322]

PEARSON, JOHN, a mariner in Anstruther Easter, a sasine, 1654. [NRS.RS31.275]

PEARSON, ROBERT, was admitted as a baker burgess and guilds-brother of Cupar on 14 November 1798. [CPR]

PEARSON, THOMAS, a school-master in Kettle, a deed, 1752. [NRS.RD4.178/2.389]

PEIRSON, JOHN, born 1789, son of John and Margaret Pierson, a Lieutenant of the 3rd Native Infantry Regiment, died at Cannanore in the East Indies, on 18 February 1812. [Kettle gravestone]

PEAT, JOHN, a burgess of Anstruther, a sasine, 1632. [NRS.RS31.X.133]

PEATIE, ALEXANDER, a citizen of St Andrews, a sasine, 1645. [NRS.RS31.XV.126]

PEEBLES, CHRISTIAN, spouse of John Landells in Muircambus, a sasine, 1621. [NRS.RS31.III.253]

PENTLAND, GEORGE, chaplain of St Marniff's Chapel in Crail Castle, a sasine, 1620. [NRS.RS31.III.30]

PETRIE, WILLIAM, schoolmaster of Kemback, 1690. [SHS.4.2]

PHILIP, ALEXANDER, a ship-builder in Burntisland, a deed, 1752. [NRS.RD4.178/2.583]

PHILIP, JAMES, portioner of Berriehole, Lindores, 1657. [RGS.X.622]

PHILIP, JOHN, in Newburgh, 1657. [RGS.X.622]

PHILIP, JOHN, in Wester Bowhill, Auchtertool, a bond, 1683. [NRS.GD1.49.32]

PHILIP, MICHAEL, son of James Philip, was granted the land of Grange of Lindores in 1657. [RGS.X.622]

PHILIPS, ROBERT, a sailor in Leven, aboard the <u>Rising Sun</u> bound for Darien in 1699, testament, 1707, Comm. Edinburgh. [NRS]

PHILIP, THOMAS, a timberman in Dubbieside, husband of Margaret Anderson, a sasine, 1655. [NRS.RS31.XIX.325]

PHILLIPSHILL, JOHN, the younger, a merchant in Glasgow, was admitted as a burgess of Auchtermuchty on 3 July 1743. [ABR]

PHILP, CHRISTIAN, born 1708, wife of James Wilkie, died 18 December 1746. [Auchtermuchty gravestone]

PHILP, DAVID, of Kippo, a physician, born 1569, died 6 January 1640. [Crombie Old Church gravestone]; a sasine 1617. [NRS.RS31.I.101]

PHILP, GEORGE, in Dunfermline, a deed, 1751. [NRS.RD3.211/2.13]

PHILP, ISABEL, daughter of John Philp the clerk of the court in Newburgh, 1620. [NRS.E107.64]

PHILP, JAMES, the younger, portioner of Berryhole, Lindores, 1620. [NRS.E107.64]

PHILP, JAMES, born 1749, late of Byrehills, died 1800, husband of Mary Bell, born 1754, died 1824. [St Andrews gravestone]

PHILP, JOHN, in Kilconquhar, 1731. [NRS.GD62.325]

PHIN, Major DAVID, of Whythill and Hillside, husband of Jean Duncan, a sasine, 1645. [NRS.RS31.XV.154]

PIERSON, WILLIAM, MA, minister at Dunfermline from 1666 until 1676. [F.V.28]

PIRIE, ANDREW, a skipper in St Monance, husband of Agnes Binning, sasine, 1628. [NRS.RS31.VII.253]

PIRIE, JOHN, a mariner in St Monance, a sasine, 1627. [NRS.RS31.VII.253]

PITBLADO, CHRISTIAN, relict of Alexander Spence a shoemaker in St Andrews, a contract, 1739. [NRS.B65.5.4/330]

PITBLADO, DAVID, in St Andrews, a bond, 1707. [NRS.B65.5.2/42]

PITBLADO, PETER, a maltman, portioner of Nethertoun of Collenquhies, husband of Eupham Douglas, a sasine, 1635. [NRS.RS31.XI.180]

PITCAIRN, CHARLES, son of Andrew Pitcairn, a groom of the chamber and falconer to the king, a sasine, 1641. [NRS.RS31.XIII.186]

PITCAIRN, EUPHANE, daughter of John Pitcairn in St Andrews, testament, 1727, Comm. St Andrews. [NRS]

PITCAIRN, HARRY, a wright in Newburgh, a sasine, 1620. [NRS.RS31.II.34]

PITCAIRN, JAMES, minister at Burntisland from 1688 until 1691. [F.V.82]

PITCAIRN, JOHN, of Unstoun, sold the lands of Unstoun in the parish of Scoonie to his brother Alexander Pitcairn of Kilmukis on 30 March 1654, sasine dated 4 April 1654, Sale confirmed by Oliver Cromwell on 21 July 1654. [RGS.X.311]

PITCAIRN, JOHN, born 1722 in Dysart, son of Reverend David Pitcairn and his wife Catharine Hamilton, a Major of the Royal Marines, died at the Battle of Bunker's Hill in Massachusetts, on 19 April 1775. [F.5.87]

PITCAIRN, ROBERT, born 1737, from Newburgh, a tavern-keeper in Spanish Town, Jamaica, by 1780, died 22 July 1799. [Spanish Town gravestone] [NRS.GD1.675.113]

PITCAIRN, THOMAS, a feuar in Kinnimont, a deed, 1752.
[NRS.RD4.178/2.358]

PITSCOTTIE, COLIN, a sailor, son of John Pitscottie of Craigduchie,
aboard the Rising Sun bound for Darien in 1699, testament, 1707,
Comm. Edinburgh. [NRS]

PITTENDREICH, DAVID, born 1798, son of Robert Pittendreich and
his wife Catherine Gay, died off the coast of Africa in 1833. [Cupar
gravestone]

PITTILLOCK, NATHAN, a skipper in Elie, was admitted as a burgess
of St Andrews on 16 August 1760. [SABR]

PLAYFAIR, CHARLES, born 7 June 1795, son of Reverend James
Playfair and his wife Grizel Duncan in Bendochy, died in America.
[F.5.254]

PLAYFAIR, GEORGE, born 1782, Inspector General of Hospitals in
Bengal, husband of Jessie Ross, died on 26 November 1846. [St
Andrews gravestone]

PLAYFAIR, WILLIAM DAVIDSON, born 1784, a Lieutenant Colonel
in the Service of the Honorable East India Company in Bengal,
died on 31 January 1852. [St Andrews gravestone]

PORTER, THOMAS, a sailor in Burntisland, testament, 1801,
Comm. St Andrews. [NRS]

PORTEFIELD, LAURENCE, son of William Porterfield a shoemaker,
was admitted as a burgess of St Andrews on 13 August 1774.
[SABR]

PORTERFIELD, WILLIAM, a shoemaker in St Andrews in 1775, [St
Andrews gravestone]; in St Andrews in October 1798.
[NRS.E326.15.31]

POTTER, ROBERT, a skipper in Leven, son of William Potter, 1702. [NRS.RS31.80.417]

PRESTON, Lieutenant General Sir GEORGE, of Valleyfield, deeds, 1752. [NRS.RD3.211/2.443; RD4.178/1.577]

PRIDE, DAVID, born 1757, a shoemaker in Fife, emigrated aboard the Friendship bound for Philadelphia in 1775. [TNA.T47.12]

PRINGLE, JOHN, a barber in St Andrews, was admitted as a burgess of St Andrews on 15 August 1755. [SABR]

PRINGLE, JOHN, a meal-maker in St Andrews, was admitted as a burgess of St Andrews on 9 May 1765. [SABR]

PROPHET, JOHN, schoolmaster of St Monance, 1690. [SHS.4.2]

PRYDE, DANIEL, in Ferryport-on-Craig, 1795. [NRS.CH2.150.4 .191]

PRYDE, DAVID, tenant in Brownhills, St Andrews, testament, 1706, Comm. St Andrews. [NRS]

PRYDE, DAVID, born 1757, a shoemaker from Fife, emigrated via Leith aboard the Friendship bound for Philadelphia, Pennsylvania, on 9 May 1775. [TNA.T47.12]

PRYDE, JAMES, was served heir to his father Alexander Pryde a blacksmith in St Andrews on 8 June 1642. [NRS.Retours.Fife.1448]

PRYDE, JAMES, a weaver in Strathmiglo, a Covenanter transported aboard the St Michael of Scarborough to the West Indies in 1678. [RPCS.VI.76]

PRIDE, JAMES, a maltman in St Andrews, testament, 1702. Comm. St Andrews. [NRS]

PRIDE, JAMES, a candle-maker in Leslie, a deed, 1749. [NRS.GD1.392.166]

PRIDE, THOMAS, in East Grange of St Andrews, testament, 1709, Comm. St Andrews. [NRS]

PUNT, JOHN, a meal-maker in St Andrews, was admitted as a burgess of St Andrews on 17 December 1768. [SABR]

RAE, LINDSAY, a tiler in St Andrews, was admitted as a burgess of St Andrews on 9 September 1773. [SABR]

RAIT, DAVID, born 1772 in Fife, died in St Andrews, New Brunswick, on 8 May 1838. [St Andrews Standard: 12.5.1838]

RAMSAY, DAVID, in Balmerino, 1653. [RGS.X.106]

RAMSAY, DAVID, son of Andrew Ramsay of Abbotshall, a deed, 1749. [NRS.RD3.172.517]

RAMSAY, GEORGE, schoolmaster of Markinch, 1690. [SHS.4.2]

RAMSAY, GEORGE, eldest son of George Ramsay a meal-maker and burgess of St Andrews, was admitted as a burgess of St Andrews on 25 January 1755. [SABR]

RAMSAY, HENRY, Regent of the Old College of St Andrews, testaments, 1744-1745, Comm. St Andrews. [NRS]

RAMSAY, ISABEL, born 1535, wife of Alexander Mathiu of Kirkton of Balmerino, died 8 October 1596. [Balmerino gravestone]

RAMSAY, JAMES, in West Miln of Auchtermuchty, was admitted as a burgess of Auchtermuchty on 5 May 1738. [ABR]

RAMSAY, JOHN, a mariner who was admitted as a burgess of St Andrews on 3 March 1763. [SABR]

RAMSAY, JOHN, son of David Ramsay and his wife Helen Wemyss, a shop-keeper in Charleston, South Carolina, probate 20 July 1734, South Carolina. [Caledonian Mercury#2326]

RAMSAY, JOHN, son of George Ramsay a meal-maker burgess, was admitted as a burgess of St Andrews on 8 January 1771. [SABR]

RAMSAY, ROBERT, in St Andrews, son of James Ramsay a weaver burgess of St Andrews, was admitted as a burgess of St Andrews on 2 August 1759. [SABR]

RAMSAY, THOMAS, master of the James of Kirkcaldy trading with Norway in 1719. [NRS.CE52.1.3]

RAMSAY, WILLIAM, born 1725, Deacon of the Weavers of St Andrews, died 19 June 1801, husband of Helen Gourlay, born 1717, died 9 July 1795. [St Andrews gravestone]

RANKEILLOR, DAVID, a merchant in St Andrews, testament, 1732, Comm. St Andrews. [NRS]

RANKEILLER, THOMAS, a sailor in Wemyss, son of James Rankeiller, aboard the Rising Sun bound for Darien in 1699, testament, 1708, Comm. Edinburgh. [NRS]

RANKINE, PATRICK, was served heir to his brother James Rankine portioner of Auchtermuchtie, on 6 January 1687. [NRS.Retours.Fife.1451]

RATTRAY, JANET, in St Andrews, testament, 1734, Comm. St Andrews. [NRS]

RATTRAY, PATRICK, a burgess of Newburgh by 1740. [NBR]

REDDIE, ALEXANDER, born 1687, tenant of Nethertown, died 31 March 1745. [Beath gravestone]

REDDIE, JAMES, tacksman of Dysart Coal Works, a deed, 1794. [NRS.B21.5.3/331]

REDDIE, JOHN, master of the Europa of Dysart trading with Memel in 1767. [NRS.E504.27.3]

REID, ALEXANDER, master of the Friendship of Anstruther trading with Danzig in 1749, [NRS.E504.3.3]; arrived in Anstruther from Virginia on 14 March 1766. [NRS.E504.3.3]

REID, ALEXANDER, a thatcher, second son of William Reid a thatcher in St Andrews, was admitted as a burgess of St Andrews on 14 March 1755. [SABR]

REID, ALEXANDER, a merchant in Dysart, was admitted as a burgess of St Andrews on 4 July 1769. [SABR]

REID, ALEXANDER, a meal-maker, son of James Reid a wright in St Andrews, was admitted as a burgess of St Andrews on 8 September 1773. [SAB]

REID, ALEXANDER, a slater in St Andrews, husband of Janet Millar, a dispensation, 4 September 1782. [NRS.B65.5.6/115; B65.22.35]

REID, ANDREW, master of the Hawk of Anstruther whaling off Greenland from 1758 to 1762. [NRS.E504.3.3]; master of the Friendship of Anstruther bound for Virginia in 1769; also of the Friendship of Cellardyke bound for Grenada in 1772, 1773, 1774, 1775. [NRS.E504.22.15/17/18/19/20]

REID, ANDREW, born 1798, son of William Reid, in the service of the Honorable East India Company, died in Chittagong, Bengal, on 16 MARCH 1822. [Creich gravestone]

REID, DAVID, a tenant in Craigrothie, was admitted as a burgess of St Andrews on 6 March 1756. [SABR]

REID, DAVID, born 1764, a fisherman in Cellardyke, husband of Margaret Boytar, died on 14 July 1830. [Kilrenny gravestone]

REID, JOHN, master of the Defiance of Anstruther trading with Danzig, Gothenburg, Spain and Zealand, in 1749 to 1753. [NRS.E504.3.3]; was admitted as a burgess of St Andrews on 3 November 1760. [SABR]

REID, JOHN, a thatcher, son of William Reid a thatcher in St Andrews, was admitted as a burgess of St Andrews on 14 March 1755. [SABR]

REID, JOHN, son of John Reid in Culross, a thief who was transported to America in 1763. [NRS.B59.26.11.6.41]

REIDIE, DAVID, a seaman in Burntisland, settled at Port Nelson, Hudson Bay, in 1683. [HBRS.9.90]

REITH, ANNE, a fraudster in Pittenweem, wife of Alexander Morton, was transported to the colonies in 1774. [NRS.B59.26.11.6.20]

RENWICK, HENRY, born 1730, tenant of Denbrae, died 11 April 1804, spouse Jane......, born 1723, died 22 October 1789. [St Andrews gravestone]

RICHARD, AGNES, daughter of the late David Richard former Deacon of the Weavers of St Andrews, a marriage contract, 1752. [NRS.B65.22.40]

RICHARD, MELVILLE, son of William Richard and his wife Catherine Bell, master of the Jane of Glasgow died at Black River, Jamaica, on 26 July 1817. [St Andrews gravestone]

RICHARD, ROBERT, born 1706, a feur in Strathkinness, died 1777, husband of Catherine Morris, born 1718, died 1794. [St Andrews gravestone]

RICHARDSON, ANDREW, in Ridie Leys, a husbandman, died 1736. [Auchtermuchty gravestone]

RICHARDSON, BEATRIX, relict of James Richardson portioner of Auchtermuchty, deed, 1760. [NRS.B5.4.1/12]

RICHARDSON, DAVID, a merchant in Auchtermuchty, was admitted as a burgess of St Andrews on 9 October 1770. [SABR]

RICHARDSON, DAVID, a writer in Auchtermuchty, his wife Grizel Ballingal, and daughter Ann, a deed, 1791. [NRS.GD1.675.64]

RIGG, WILLIAM, a surgeon apothecary in Cupar, a deed, 1736. [NRS.RD2.211/2.505]

RIND, ANDREW, a ballmaker in St Andrews, a bond, 1641 [HL#747]

RINTOUL, JOHN, a merchant in Kirkcaldy, trading with Boston and the West Indies in 1783. [NRS.CS17.1.2]

RITCHIE, ALEXANDER, master of the Nancy of Burntisland from Kirkcaldy to Charleston, South Carolina, in 1753. [South Carolina Gazette, 24.12.1753][TNA.CO5.510][NRS.E504.20.3]; testament, 1808, Comm. St Andrews. [NRS]

RITCHIE, DAVID, servant to Harry Rymer minister at Carnbie, a charter witness, 21 July 1654. [RGS.X.311]

RITCHIE, JAMES, in St Andrews, was admitted as a burgess of St Andrews on 26 November 1770. [SABR]

RITCHIE, JOHN, a soldier from Kirkcaldy, a Jacobite who was transported to the colonies in 1747. [P.3.274]

RITCHIE, JOHN, in St Andrews, was admitted as a burgess of St Andrews on 15 May 1755. [SABR]

RITCHIE, JOHN, born 1795, captain of the Caledonian of Dundee, died in Elsinore, Denmark, on 18 June 1842. [St Andrews gravestone]

RITCHIE, NINIAN, a meal-maker in St Andrews, was admitted as a burgess of St Andrews on 30 December 1765. [SABR]

RITCHIE, ROBERT, son of Robert Ritchie and his wife Janet Mill in Dysart, died aboard HMS Orford in the East Indies pre-1775. A dispensation. [NRS.B21.5.2/243]

RITCHIE, ROBERT, from Fife, was admitted as a burgher of St Eustatia in the Dutch West Indies on 21 November 1780. [TNA.CO318.8.84V]

ROBERTSON, ALEXANDER, a weaver in St Andrews, was admitted as a burgess of St Andrews on 31 January 1757. [SABR]

ROBERTSON, ANDREW, a skipper from Anstruther, trading in Konigsberg in 1597. [KT.152.135]

ROBERTSON, DAVID, born 1598, a smith, died on 9 November 1652. [Culross West gravestone]

ROBERTSON, DAVID, second son of David Robertson a burgess of St Andrews, was admitted as a burgess of St Andrews on 29 December 1757. [SABR]

ROBERTSON, GILBERT, shore-master at Methil, a deed, 1754. [NRS.B21.5.1/223]

ROBERTSN, JAMES, a bailie of Burntisland, 1689. [RPCS.XIV.455]

ROBERTSON, JAMES, son of James Robertson a guilds-brother of St Andrews, was admitted as a burgess of St Andrews on 1 September 1769. [SABR]

ROBERTSON, JAMES, of Dennork, was admitted as a burgess of St Andrews on 28 March 1771. [SABR]

ROBERTSON, JAMES, servant to Durham of Largo, was admitted as a burgess of St Andrews in 1774. [SABR]

ROBERTSON, JAMES, from Newbigging, a Lieutenant General, probate 22 March 1788, New York; probate 5 April 1788, New Jersey. [New Jersey Archives, lib.38/520]

ROBERTSON, JAMES, born 1796, a merchant in Charleston, South Carolina, was naturalised there in 1823. [NARA.M1183.1]

ROBERTSON, JOHN, a seaman in Burntisland, aboard the St Andrew bound for Darien in 1698, testament, 1707, Comm. Edinburgh. [NRS]

ROBERTSON, PATRICK, a meal-maker, eldest son of William Robertson a meal-maker burgess of St Andrews, was admitted as a burgess of St Andrews on 4 January 1771. [SABR]

ROBERTSON, THOMAS, third son of William Robertson a meal-maker burgess of St Andrews, was admitted as a burgess of St Andrews on 4 January 1771. [SABR]

ROBERTSON WILLIAM, a physician in Burntisland, with wife Elizabeth Allen, and children William born 1683 and Elizabeth born 1685, emigrated to East New Jersey, settled in Monmouth County in 1690. [NJSA.EJD.D209]
[NRS.Quaker Records.E11.4/15.336]

ROBERTSON, WILLIAM, a meal-maker, second son of William Robertson a meal-maker burgess of St Andrews, was admitted as a burgess of St Andrews on 4 January 1771. [SABR]

ROBIN, HENRY, graduated MA from Edinburgh University in 1693, minister at Burntisland from 1714 until 1718, died in January 1734. [F.V.82]

RODGER, ALEXANDER, in St Andrews, was admitted as a burgess of St Andrews on 4 August 1759. [SABR]

RODGER, JAMES, a skipper in St Andrews, testament, 1807, Comm. St Andrews. [NRS]

ROGERSON, ALBERT, a skipper from Anstruther, trading in Konigsberg in 1597. [KT.127.145]

ROGERSON, ANDREW, a skipper from Anstruther, trading in Konigsberg in 1597. [KT.127.143]

ROGERSON, ROBERT, a skipper from Anstruther, trading in Konigsberg in 1602. [KT.127.143]

ROLLAND, HENRY, son of James Rolland in Culross, a carpenter who settled in Charleston, South Carolina, before 1774. [NRS.CS16.1.137]

ROLLO, ROBERT, schoolmaster of Leslie, a sasine, 1623. [NRS.RS30.4.344]

RONALDSON, HENRY, a mariner aboard the Blessing of Kirkcaldy who was captured by Turkish pirates in July 1632 between La Rochelle in France and Scotland, a prisoner in Algiers. [RPCS.V.142]

RORIE, ALEXANDER, in East Wemyss, husband of Catherine Massoun, a sasine, 1608. [NRS.RS30.XI.9]

ROSS, AGNES, born 1715, a spinner in Kirkcaldy, emigrated to North Carolina in 1736. [CLRO/AIA]

ROSS, ANDREW, a skipper from Anstruther, trading in Konigsberg in 1597. [KT.378.202]

ROSS, DONALD, a guilds-brother, was admitted as a burgess of St Andrews on 4 August 1769. [SABR]

ROSS, WILLIAM, a skipper from Leven, trading in Konigsberg in 1596. [KT.367.203]

ROSS, WILLIAM, a skipper in Markinch, testament, 1617, Comm. St Andrews. [NRS]

ROW, WILLIAM, schoolmaster of Crail, 1690. [SHS.4.2]

ROWAN, ALEXANDER, was admitted as a burgess of Crail in 1756. [CBR]

ROWAN, WILLIAM, of Gaslee, was jointly granted the lands and barony of Cardoun in the parish of Auchterderran in November 1657. [RGS.X.627]

ROXBURGH, ANDREW, son of John Roxburgh a beadle, was admitted as a burgess of Dunfermline on 31 July 1790. [DM]

ROXBURGH, WILLIAM, a merchant and bailie of Inverkeithing, father of Jean, Ann, Janet and Margaret, a deed, 1792. [NRS.B34.20.36]

ROXBURGH, WILLIAM, second son of William Roxburgh a merchant and magistrate of Inverkeithing and his second wife Margaret Greig, an officer of the Royal Navy, later in Russian service, died in 1780s. [HIR.487]

ROY, JAMES, born in Fife, died 25 July 1818 in Augusta, Georgia. [Colonial Museum and Savanna Advertiser, 4 August 1818]

RUNSHIEMAN, WILLIAM, a mariner in Crail, husband of Catherine Wishart, born 1722 – died 1753, drowned when fishing on 21 January 1765. [Crail gravestone]

RUSSELL, JAMES, a mariner in Philadelphia, Pennsylvania, a sasine, 1791. [NRS.RS31.2943]

RUSSEL, JOHN, born 1677, farmer in Buchlyvie, died 18 June 1743. [Aberdour gravestone]

RUSSELL, THOMAS, schoolmaster of Kettle, 1690. [SHS.4.2]

RUSSELL, WILLIAM, a meal-maker in St Andrews, was admitted as a burgess of St Andrews on 8 August 1765. [SABR]

RUSSELL, ..., born 21 November 1781, Lieutenant Colonel of the 7th Native Infantry in the Service of the Honorable East India Company, died 10 July 1839. [Pittenweem gravestone]

RUSSELL, JAMES, born 23 April 1708, son of James Russell and his wife Anne Wightman in Kingseat, Slipperfield, settled in Nottingham, Prince George County, Maryland, in 1730. [Maryland Historical Magazine.72.165]

RUSSELL, WILLIAM, born 1751, a farmer from Cupar, emigrated aboard the Glasgow Packet bound for Salem, New England, in 1775. [TNA.T47.12]

RUTHERFORD, ANDREW, son of John Rutherford a skipper in Kirkcaldy and his wife Isobel Lumsdaine, testament, 1770, Comm. Edinburgh. [NRS]

RUTHERFORD, DAVID, from Cupar, an assessor of the Scots Court in Veere, Zealand, in 1731. [NRS.RH11.2.1]

RUTHERFORD, GEORGE, a skipper in Dysart, husband of Girzel Barclay, a deed, 1775. [NRS.B21.5.2/231]; master of the Christian of Dysart trading with Hamburg and Bremen in 1762, [NRS.E504.3.3]; master of the George of Dysart trading with Wiborg in 1766-1767. [NRS.E504.27.3]

RUTHERFORD, LUMSDEN, a skipper in Dysart, testament, 1803, Comm. St Andrews. [NRS]

RUTHERFORD, THOMAS, born 1766, son of Thomas Rutherford and his wife Janet Meldrum in Kirkcaldy, educated at Glasgow University, settled in Virginia in 1784, died 1790.

RYMER, JAMES, born in St Andrews, settled in South Carolina in 153, a minister, died in Walterborough, South Carolina, in 1755. [South Carolina Gazette, 10 July 1755]

RYMER, PRIMROSE, a writer in Cupar, was admitted as a burgess of St Andrews on 24 October 1761. [SABR]

RYMONT, WILLIAM, a burgess of Newburgh by 1740. [NBR]

SALMOND, PETER, a boatman in Burntisland, a deed, 1765. [NRS.B9.7.1/121]

SALMOND, ROBERT, master of the Grizel of Inverleven trading with Christiansands, Norway, in 1750. [NRS.E504.3.3]; master of the Betty of Methil bound from Kirkcaldy to Boston, New England, in 1753. [NRS.CE63; E504.20.3]

SANDERSON, WILLIAM, an Ensign, from Kinghorn, died in Darien in 1699, testament, 1707, Comm. Edinburgh. [NRS]

SANDILANDS, Sir JAMES, of St Monans, was admitted as a burgess of Dundee on 7 November 1633. [DBR]

SANDS, JAMES, a merchant in Gothenborg, Sweden, son and heir of John Sands a merchant in Culross, a deed, 1726. [NRS.B12.5.1/153]

SANDS, WILLIAM, a sailor in Dunfermline, aboard the Rising Sun bound for Darien in 1699, testament, 1707, Comm. Edinburgh. [NRS]

SANDS, WILLIAM, a maltman burgess of Culross, a bond, 1741. [NRS.B12.5.2/52-53]

SCHANK, MARTIN, MA, minister at Auchtertool from 1694 to 1697. [F.V.78]

SCOTLAND, HENRY, son of Henry Scotland a burgess, was admitted as a burgess of Dunfermline on 23 May 1797. [DM]

SCOTLAND, JOHN, a merchant in Dunfermline, a deed, 1752. [NRS.RD2.172.233]

SCOTLAND, WILLIAM, a skipper in Kincardine, husband of Elisabeth Meiklejohn, a bond, 1794. [NRS.B12.5.4/331-339]

SCOTT, ANDREW, a ship-builder in Burntisland, 1798. [NRS.AC7.72]

SCOTT, CHRISTIAN, a servant in Kirkcaldy, daughter of James Scott, guilty of infanticide, transported to the colonies in August 1762. [NRS.HCR.I.94]

SCOTT, EUPHEMIA, daughter of George Scott of Pitlochie, wife of John Johnston, bound for East New Jersey aboard the Henry and Francis in 1685. [Insh.178]

SCOTT, GEORGE, of Pitlochie, emigrated aboard the Henry and Francis bound for East New Jersey in 1685, died at sea, testament, 1692, Comm. Edinburgh. [NRS]

SCOTT, ISABEL, daughter of John Scott tenant in Newburn, and spouse of David Carstairs, versus said David Carstairs, process of separation and aliment, 1791. [NRS.CC8.6.874]

SCOTT, JAMES, a Customs Officer in St Andrews, was admitted as a burgess of St Andrews on 10 November 1759. [SABR]

SCOTT, JOHN, a mariner aboard the Blessing of Kirkcaldy who was captured by Turkish pirates in July 1632 between La Rochelle in France and Scotland, a prisoner in Algiers. [RPCS.V.142]

SCOTT, JOHN, minister at Auchtertool from 1787 until 1797. [F.V.79]

SCOTT, JOHN, a farmer in Balbuthie, Colinsburgh, 1798. [NRS.AC7.72]

SCOTT, JOHN, son of John Scott, [1750-1813] and his wife Jane French [1750-1816], died in America. [Monimail gravestone]

SCOTT, JOHN, in Demerara, son of John Scott a merchant in Kincardine-on-Forth, a deed, 1802. [NRS.RD3.295.657]

SCOTT, PHILIP, a skipper in Pittenweem, testament, 1805, Comm. St Andrews. [NRS]

SCOTT, THOMAS, born 1752, died 8 November 1775, son of John Scott a tenant in Oldmuirs. [Ferry-port-on-Craig gravestone]

SCOTT, THOMAS, a Major in the Service of the Honorable East India Company, a sasine, 1782. [NRS.RS31.1782]

SCOTT, WILLIAM, of Elie, father of William Scott, a charter, 1602. [NRS.B9.14.22]

SCOTT, WILLIAM, from Burntisland, a mariner aboard HMS Burford and HMS Coronation, probate 1691, PCC. [TNA]

SCOTT, WILLIAM, was admitted as a pewterer burgess of Cupar on 18 September 1767. [CBR]

SCRYMGEOUR, ALEXANDER, of Birkhill, Balmerino, 1778. [NRS.E326.3.15]

SCRYMGEOUR, HENRY, late of Jamaica, youngest son of David Scrymgeour of Birkhill in 1793. [NRS.NRAS.783/9]

SCRYMGEOUR, JOHN, minister at Kinghorn, husband of Grisel Forrest, a sasine, 1634.   [NRS.RS31.X.413]

SEATON, DAVID, schoolmaster of Auchterderran, 1690. [SHS.4.2]

SETON, GEORGE, a sailor in Burntisland, son of John Seton, aboard the St Andrew bound for Darien in 1698, testament, 1707, Comm. Edinburgh. [NRS]

SETON, JOHN, son of David Seton of Parbroath and his wife Mary Gray, emigrated via London to Virginia on 7 August 1635. [TNA.E157.20]

SETON, JOHN, late from Jamaica, in Collessie, a sasine, 1782. [NRS.RS31.268]

SELKIRK, ALEXANDER, a burgess of Kilrenny, a sasine, 1648. [NRS.RS31.XVI.243]

SELKIRK, JOHN, in Kennoway, a sasine 1650. [NRS.RS31.XVII.241]

SELKIRK, WILLIAM, son of Alexander Selkirk, a sculptor in Buckhaven, a sasine, 1628. [NRS.RS31.VII.439]

SHARP, DANIEL, a vintner in Ferryport-on-Craig, a deed, 1696. [NRS.RD4.79.564]

SHEPHERD, ALEXANDER, born 1711, died 1776, husband of Ann Baillie, born 1729, died 1804. [Forgan gravestone]

SHEPHERD, THOMAS, born 1739, tenant in Balmerino Mill, died in December 1796, husband of Jean Walker, born 1745, died September 1797. [Balmerino gravestone]

SHIELDS, ALEXANDER, a minister in St Andrews, a chaplain on the Darien Expedition in 1699, died in Port Royal, Jamaica, in 1700. [F.7.655]

SHINE, Captain ALEXANDER, a skipper in Crail, was admitted as a burgess of St Andrews on 2 February 1770. [SABR]

SHOOLBRED, JOHN, a baker in Auchtermuchty, a deed, 1760. [NRS.B5.4.1/8]

SHOOLBRED, JOHN, a tailor in Chamber Street, Dunfermline, was admitted as a burgess of Dunfermline on 13 March 1810. [DM]

SIBBALD, ALEXANDER, was admitted as a shoemaker burgess of Cupar on 24 September 1766. [CBR]

SIBBALD, CHARLES, a gentleman in St Andrews, a Jacobite in 1745. [SHS.8.68/352]

SIBBALD, CHARLES, a meal-maker in St Andrews, was admitted as a burgess of St Andrews on 28 February 1756. [SABR]

SIBBALD, JAMES, schoolmaster of Monimail, a deed, 1668, [NRS.RD4.20.143]; schoolmaster of Abernethy, 1698. [SUL.ms36220/338]

SIBBALD, JAMES, a brewer in Auchtermuchtie, and his wife Jean Aitken, a process of aliment, 1775. [NRS.CC8.6.557]

SIBBALD, JOHN, from Kirkcaldy, a merchant in Philadelphia, 1772. [NRS.B41.7.8/187]

SIMMONS, ALEXANDER, a soldier from Anstruther, married Marieken Jansen in Rotterdam in the Netherlands in 1588. [Rotterdam Marriage Register]

SIMMERS, WILLIAM, a tailor in Crail, son of James Simmers a tailor in Crail, 1774. [NRS.B10.5.1/84]

SIMPSON, ALEXANDER, master of the Christian of Kirkcaldy trading between Kirkcaldy and Holland in 1682. [NRS.E72.9.13]

SIMPSON, ALEXANDER, a mariner in Dysart, aboard the St Andrew bound for Darien in 1698, testament, 1707, Comm. Edinburgh. [NRS]

SIMPSON, DAVID, and his wife Marie Lentron, from Dysart, then in Stockholm, Sweden, a deed, 1688. [NRS.RD2.69.311]

SIMPSON, JAMES, a skipper in Dysart, testament, 1710, Comm. Edinburgh. [NRS]

SIMSON, JAMES, a surgeon in St Andrews, was admitted as a burgess of St Andrews on 5 February 1760. [SABR]

SIMSON, JAMES, a merchant in Falkland, a bond, 1778. [NRS.CS181.1764.7]

SIMPSON, MARGARET, born 1752, a servant in Dunfermline, emigrate to Philadelphia aboard the Friendship in 1775. [NRS.T47.12]

SIMSON, ROBERT, a meal-maker in St Andrews, was admitted as a burgess of St Andrews on 13 November 1755. [SABR]

SIMSON, THOMAS, son of John Simson of Balchrystie, died in Darien in 1699, testament, 1708, Comm. Edinburgh. [NRS]

SIMPSON, WILLIAM, son of Reverend Gilbert Simpson in Kingsbarns, was apprenticed to Charles Duncan a goldsmith burgess of Edinburgh in 1713, [ERA]; IN 1726, as a goldsmith in Crail he was admitted as a burgess of St Andrews. [SABR]

SINCLAIR, MATTHEW, a merchant from Dysart, in Veere, Zealand, in 1728. [NRS.RH11/2]

SMART, DAVID, a founder from Strathmiglo, settled in New York before 1775. [NRS.S/H.7.11.1775]

SMART, JAMES, schoolmaster of Newburgh, 1689. [SHS.4.2] [SUL.ms36220/351]

SMART, JAMES, born 1687 in Dysart, a sailor aboard the Angelica bound from Torbay, England, to Virginia on 22 August 1707. [TNA.HCA.Lamb versus Murrin, 1708]

SMART, LAWRENCE, from Dunfermline, was admitted as a citizen of Cracow in 1598. [BPL.279]

SMART, THOMAS, son of George Smart a carter in Dysart, apprenticed to George Mavor a mason in Dysart, for 3 years in 1792. [NRS.B21.5.3/361]

SMITH, ADAM, born 1723 in Kirkcaldy, son of Adam Smith a Writer to the Signet, an Economist and author of 'The Wealth of Nations', died in Edinburgh on 17 July 1790.

SMITHE, ANDREW, was served heir to his father William Smithe portioner of Northfod on 28 November 1640. [NRS.Retours.Fife.1447]

SMITH, DAVID, born 1796, son of Robert Smith and his wife Janet Henderson, a merchant in New Orleans, died in Perth on 27 December 1882. [Logie, Fife, gravestone]

SMITH, JAMES, a meal-maker, only son of James Smith a meal-maker burgess of St Andrews, was admitted as a burgess of St Andrews on 15 December 1757. [SABR]

SMITH, JEAN, born 1754, a servant in Dunfermline, emigrated to Philadelphia aboard the Friendship in 1775. [TNA.T47.12]

SMITH, JOHN, MA, minister at Burntisland from 1643 to 1648. [F.V.81]

SMITH, JOHN, master of the Jean of Ely bound for Charleston in 1765. [NRS.E504.22.12]

SMITH, JOHN, master of the Jane of Anstruther bound for South Carolina in 1766. [TNA.CO5.511]

SMITH, JOHN, born 1755, a weaver in Kirkton, died 14 February 1819, husband of Katherine Fowles, born 1754, died 30 September 1828. [Balmerino gravestone]

SMITH, JOHN, born 1793, son of David Smith and his wife Euphame Ramsay, died in Jamaica in 1820. [Dunnikier gravestone]

SMITH, ROBERT, master of the Jamaica Packet of Burntisland bound for Antigua in 1774. [TNA.T47.12]

SMITH, ROBERT, born 1798, son of David Smith and his wife Euphame Murray, died in Calcutta on 28 September 1844. [Dunnikier gravestone]

SMITH, SIMON, schoolmaster of Crail, a sasine, 1620. [NRS.RS30.2.237]

SMITH, THOMAS, master of the Jamaica Packet of Burntisland bound for the Carolinas in 1775. [NRS.E504.20.8]

SMITH, WILLIAM, was admitted as a hammerman burgess of Cupar on 30 September 1769. [CBR]

SOMERVILLE, WILLIAM, a sailor in Culross, husband of Isobel Dalgleish, aboard the St Andrew bound for Darien in 1698, testament, 1707, Comm. Edinburgh. [NRS]

SORLIE, WILLIAM, a skipper in Kincardine, a deed, 1788. [NRS.B12.5.4/126-132]

SPARK, PATRICK, a surgeon in St Andrews, was admitted as a burgess of St Andrews on 9 April 1763. [SABR]

SPEARS, ROBERT, born 1700, son of Robert Spears and his wife Margaret Stewart in Bo'ness, graduated MA from Edinburgh University in 1719, minister at Burntisland from 1743 to 1777, died 14 October 1778. [F.V.83]

SPEEDIE, ROBERT, a weaver in Dunnikier, husband of Margaret Welsh, a deed, 1781. [NRS.B21.5.2/398]

SPENCE, NATHANIEL, of Lathalland, Kilconquhar, a petition, 12 September 1689. [RPCS.XIV.264]

SPENCE, ROBERT, a clockmaker in Dysart, a deed, 1800. [NRS.B21.5.4/12-15]

SPINDIE, JOHN, born 1675, a wright and a church elder, died 17 September 1742. [Balmerino gravestone]; in the Ground of Nachtane in 1717. [BA.635]

SPITTAL, ROBERT, born 1691, a shoemaker and a burgess of Culross, died 1 April 1741. [Culross Abbey gravestone]

SPITTAL, ROBERT, born 1760, died 25 June 1772. [Culross Abbey gravestone]

SPRATT, DANIEL, from Fife, settled in Urbanna, Mddlesex County, Virginia, probate 1807, Williamsburg, Virginia.

SPRATT, ROBERT BEVERLEY, settled in Urbanna, Middlesex County, Virginia, probate 1805, Williamsburg, Virginia.

STALKER, ALEXANDER, a merchant in Fossaway, was admitted as a burgess of St Andrews on 16 December 1763. [SABR]

STANEHOUSE, JOHN, in Luthrie, a tenant in the Byres of Balmerino in 1630. [BA.627]

STARK, JAMES, in Ferry-Port-on-Craig, testament, 1709, Comm. St Andrews. [NRS]

STARK, JAMES, tenant in Peasiehill, was admitted as a burgess of St Andrews on 30 December 1765. [SABR]

STARK, RICHARD, born 1661 [?], son of Richard Stark and Helen Maxwell, died 1738 {?}, husband of Helen Hardie, born 1664, died 28 October 1738. [Auchtermuchty gravestone]

STARK, THOMAS, of Bandean, 1694-1717. [BA.633]

STARK, THOMAS, born 1733, factor at Balmerino, died 16 November 1781. [Balmerino gravestone]

STARK, THOMAS, minister at Balmerino, a deed, 1761; a land-owner in Ballindean, Balmerino, in 1770. [NRS.SC20.36.10][DLS.139]

STEDMAN, ANDREW, a weaver, son of Robert Stedman a weaver, was admitted as a burgess of Dunfermline on 4 July 1797. [DM]

STEENSON, ANN, born 1756, a servant from Dysart, emigrated aboard the Friendship bound for Philadelphia in 1775. [TNA.T47.12]

STEIN, JAMES, a distiller from Kilbagie, died in Riga on 15 August 1804. [SM.66.807]

STENHOUSE, GEORGE, a sailor in Burntisland, aboard the Caledonia bound for Darien in 1698, testament, 1707, Comm. Edinburgh. [NRS]

STENHOUSE, ROBERT, son of John Stenhouse a brewer burgess, was admitted as a burgess of Dunfermline on 11 March 1791. [DM]

STEPHEN, JAMES, a bailie of Crail, was admitted as a burgess of St Andrews on 9 June 1759. [SABR]

STEPHEN, JAMES, master of the Mansfield of Crail trading with Moss in Norway in 1765. [NRS.E504.27.4]

STEVENSON, JOHN, a quartermaster in Culross, aboard the Rising Sun bound for Darien in 1699, testament, 1708, Comm. Edinburgh. [NRS]

STEWART, DAVID, a labourer in Aberdour, versus Margaret Littlejohn, daughter of David Littlejohn a shoemaker in Netherton of Dunfermline, Process of Divorce, 1790. [NRS.CC8.6.845]

STEWART, JAMES, a soldier from St Andrews, married Anneke Anthonis in Bergen op Zoom in the Netherlands in 1586. [Bergen op Zoom marriage register]

STEWART, JAMES, born 1757 in Fife, a soldier of the 78th Regiment, to America in 1778, fought at the Battle of Castine, Maine, died on 14 December 1835 in the parish of St Patrick, Charlotte County, New Brunswick. [New Brunswick Courier: 19.12.1835]

STEWART, JOHN, in St Andrews, was admitted as a burgess of St Andrews on 29 July 1760. [SABR]

STEWART, ROBERT, born 1752, died in Calcutta on 11 March 1811. [North Park gravestone, Calcutta]

STEWART, WALTER, minister at Aberdour 1635-1636. [F.V.2]

STIRK, GEORGE, of Bandene, a tenant in Boddomcraig in 1630, a heritor of Balmerino in 1658. [BA.626/631]

STIRLING, ALEXANDER, son of Alexander Stirling a weaver burgess, was admitted as a burgess of Dunfermline on 13 August 1796. [DM]

STIVENSON, ROBERT, a smith and trade councillor of Burntisland in 1689. [RPCS.XIV.455]

STRACHAN, GEORGE, a skipper in Inverkeithing, husband of Isobel Sibbald, a bond, 29 May 1638. [NRS.GD7.SEC,1/42]

STRACHAN, JAMES, Episcopalian minister of Forgan from 1678 to 1689. [SEC.137]

STRACHAN, JAMES, a mariner in Leven, husband of Agnes Smith, a sasine, 1719. [NRS.RS31.114.79]

STRACHAN, MARGARET, spouse of Thomas Cairnes portioner of Luthrie, a sasine, 1688. [NRS.GD20.1.799]

STRANG, JAMES, a sailor in Kincardine, husband of Agnes Rankine, a deed, 1788. [NRS.B12.5.4/11-125]

STRANOCH, ANDREW, master of the English School in St Andrews, was admitted as a burgess of St Andrews on 10 November 1755. [SABR]

SUNTER, JOHN, a merchant in Elie, was admitted as a burgess of St Andrews, on 30 December 1772. [SABR]

STRACHAN, JAMES, a mariner in Leven, husband of Agnes Smith, a sasine, 1719. [NRS.RS31.114.79]

STRACHAN, MARGARET, spouse of Thomas Cairnes portioner of Luthrie, a sasine, 1688. [NRS.GD20.1.799]

STRACHAN, JAMES, a mariner in Leven, husband of Agnes Smith, a sasine, 1719. [NRS.RS31.114.79]

STRACHAN, MARGARET, spouse of Thomas Cairnes portioner of Luthrie, a sasine, 1688. [NRS.GD20.1.799]

SUTHERLAND, JOHN, a vintner in Falkland, a letter, 1750. [NRS.GD1.392.170]

SUTTIE, DAVID, a mariner in Kirkcaldy, son of James Suttie and his wife Bessie Law, aboard the Caledonia bound for Darien in 1698, testament, 1707, Comm. Edinburgh. [NRS]

SUTTIE, DAVID, was admitted as a cordiner burgess of Auchtermuchty on 26 February 1748. [ABR]

SUTTIE, JOHN, born 1758, fourth son of David Suttie a shoemaker 1764. [Auchtermuchty gravestone]

SWAN, ALEXANDER, second son of Alexander Swan a baker burgess, was admitted as a burgess of St Andrews on 15 May 1755. [SABR]

SWAN, JOHN, eldest son of Alexander Swan a baker burgess, was admitted as a burgess of St Andrews on 15 May 1755. [SABR]

SWAN, ROBERT, son of James Swan a brewer and maltman in Kennoway, was apprenticed to James Hewitt a goldsmith in Edinburgh, for seven years in 1776. [ERA]

SWINTON, AGNES, born 1738, died 4 June 1804, wife of William Dow a merchant. [Ferry-Port-on-Craig gravestone]

SWINTON, JOHN, a burgess of Newburgh by 1740. [NBR]

SWINTON, WILLIAM, a tacksman in Dysart, a deed, 1776. Comm. Edinburgh. [NRS.B21.5.2/260]

SYME, ALEXANDER, son of the late William Syme of Woodhaven, a deed, 1791. [NRS.SC20.36.15]

SYME, JOHN, a cook in Earlsferry, husband of Katherine Downy, aboard the Rising Sun bound for Darien in 1699, testament, Comm. Edinburgh, 1707. [NRS]

TAILFOUR, ANDREW, schoolmaster in Fife, husband of Christian Boswell, a sasine, 1657. [NRS.RS30.20.275]

TAIT, JAMES, a seaman in Burntisland, son of William Tit and his wife Bethea Hunter, aboard the Endeavour bound for Darien in 1698, testament, 1707, Comm. Edinburgh. [NRS]

TARBIT, JOHN, a heritor of Balmerino in 1658. [BA.631]

TAYLOR, ALEXANDER, a seaman in Burntisland, aboard the St Andrew bound for Darien in 1698, testament, 1707, Comm. Edinburgh. [NRS]

TAYLOR, ANDREW, a husbandman from Kilrenny, emigrated to Jamaica in 1730. [CLRO/AIA]

TAYLOR, ARCHIBALD, from Fife, was admitted a a burgher of St Eustatia on 7 August 1780. [TNA.CO318/8/83]

TAYLOR, JOHN, born 1724, a shipmaster at Crombie Point, died in April 1800, husband of Helen Taylor, born 1720, died 15 January 1780, parents of Isabel and Francis. [Crombie gravestone]

TAYLOR, JOHN, born 1767 in Fife, a mariner, naturalised in South Carolina on 18 March 1799. [NARA.M1183/1]

TAYLOR, JOHN, born 1788, son of John Taylor, a Colonel in the service of the Honorable East India Company in Bengal, died in St Andrews on 26 July 1841. [St Andrews gravestone]

TAYLOR, NATHANIE, a minister settled in Marlborough Patuxent, died 1710. [F.7.665]

TAYLOR, ROBERT, a merchant citizen of St Andrews, and his wife Helen Arnot, a charter confirmation dated 11 November 1653, refers to their daughter Elyt Taylor, spouse of James Lentrone sometime provost of St Andrews. [RGS.X.173]

TAYLOR, ROBERT, master of the Anstruther of Anstruther trading with Scandinavia from 1766 to 1771. [NRS.E504.3.3/4]

TAYLOR, Captain THOMAS, born 1799, died in Bahia on 19 March 1850. [Anstruther Easter gravestone]

TEMPLEMAN, THOMAS, son of Thomas Templeman a weaver burgess, was admitted as a burgess of Dunfermline on 8 August 1796. [DM]

THALLAND ROBERT, and his wife Janet Kynneill, a grant of the lands of Grangemyre in Kinghorn Easter, on29 July 1624. [RGS.VIII.679]

THOMAS, ROBERT, born in Elie, married Elizabeth Attwell from Nevis, in Curacao in 7 March 1719. [Curacao Marriage Register]

THOMSON, ALEXANDER, in St Andrews, was admitted as a burgess of St Andrews on 27 September 1768. [SABR]

THOMSON, DAVID, a bailie of Inverkeithing, aboard the Unicorn bound for Darien in 1698, testament, 1707, Comm. Edinburgh. [NRS]

THOMSON, DAVID, a meal-maker, first son of David Thomson a guilds-brother of St Andrews, was admitted as a burgess of St Andrews on 16 January 1775. [SABR]

THOMSON, GEORGE, a shoemaker in St Andrews, son of William Thomson a shoemaker in St Andrews, was admitted as a burgess of St Andrews 23 January 1759. [SABR]

THOMSON, JAMES, a sailor from Aberdour, aboard the Rising Sun bound for Darien in 1699, testament, 1707, Comm. Edinburgh. [NRS]

THOMSON, JAMES, born 1683, son of James Thomson in Kinglassie, educated at St Andrews, minister at Burntisland from 1719 until 1743, he died in May 1766. [F.V.83]

THOMSON, JAMES, born 1699 in Carnbee, graduated MA from St Andrews in 1717, minister at Dunfermline from 1743 until his death on 19 October 1790. Husband of Anne Dalgleish. [F.V.32]

THOMSON, JAMES, a writer in Kirkcaldy, a deed, 1752. [NRS.RD4.178/2.288]

THOMPSON, JAMES, servant to William Durham of Largo, was admitted as a burgess of St Andrews on 5 October 1756. [SABR]

THOMSON, JAMES, third son of David Thomson a guilds-brother of St Andrews, was admitted as a burgess of St Andrews on 16 January 1775. [SABR]

THOMSON, JOHN, a merchant in Cupar, and wife Janet Rigg, a deed, 1743. [NRS.RD3.211/2.504]

THOMSON, JOHN, a Deacon of Cupar, was admitted as a burgess of St Andrews in 1774. [SABR]

THOMSON, JOHN, second son of David Thomson a guilds-brother of St Andrews, was admitted as a burgess of St Andrews on 16 January 1775. [SABR]

THOMSON, JOHN, a wig-maker in Cupar, was admitted as a burgess of St Andrews on 10 December 1774. [SABR]

THOMSON, J., master of the Collier of Inverkeithing from Bo'ness bound for New York in 1754. [NRS.CE58]

THOMSON, OLIVER, born 1757, died 16 November 1806. [Abdie gravestone]

THOMSON, PATRICK, born 1621, died 27 November 1673. [Abdie gravestone]

THOMSON, PETER, son of John Thomson in Burntisland, died in Kingston, Jamaica, in 1803. [GM.72.374]

THOMSON, ROBERT, son of William Thomson a burgess of St Andrews, was admitted as a burgess of St Andrews on 10 April 1758. [SABR]

THOMSON, ROBERT, fourth son of David Thomson a guilds-brother of St Andrews, was admitted as a burgess of St Andrews on 16 January 1775. [SABR]

THOMSON, THOMAS, master of the Alexander of Inverkeithing bound for Carolina in 1684, and 1686. [NRS.AC7.8; GD172.1585]

THOMSON, THOMAS, a fisherman in Buckhaven, testament, 1740, Comm. Edinburgh. [NRS]

THOMSON, THOMAS, son of Thomas Thomson, a baker in Dysart, and Andrew Stirling, a baker in Dysart, a contract of co-partnery, 1777, dissolved in 1781. [NRS.B21.5.2/278-281, and B21.5.2.385]

THOMSON, WILLIAM, of Nuthill, a shipmaster in Dysart, a deed, 1755. [NRS.B21.5.1/230]

THOMSON, WILLIAM, son of James Thomson jr a weaver burgess of St Andrews, was admitted as a burgess of St Andrews on 23 October 1759. [SABR]

THOMSON, WILLIAM, a Customs Surveyor in Anstruther, was admitted as a burgess of St Andrews on 3 June 1771. [SABR]

THORNE, SAMUEL, Episcopalian minister in Dunfermline 1760s. died 1765. [SEC.142]

TODD, ALEXANDER, a mariner in Dysart, died aboard HMS Ipswich, probate 1694 Prerogative Court of Canterbury. [TNA]

TODD, DAVID, a skipper from Kirkcaldy, was admitted as a burgess of Bergen, Norway, in 1692. [SAB]

TOD, GAVIN, a burgess of Newburgh by 1742. [NBR]

TOD, JOHN, born 1717, tenant in Cairniehall, died 29 November 1798, husband of Janet Williamson, born 1723, died 5 August 1784, parents of James Tod born 1750, died 11 June 1820. [Abdie gravestone]

TODD, JOHN, minister in Dunino, was admitted as a burgess of St Andrews on 30 November 1757. [SABR]

TODD, THOMAS, in Pitscottie, was admitted as a burgess of St Andrews on 20 January 1759. [SABR]

TORBAIN, JOHN, in St Andrews, was admitted as a burgess of St Andrews on 27 December 1770. [SABR]

TOSH, JAMES, from Kirkcaldy, a member of the Scots Charitable Society of Boston, New England, in 1771. [NEHGS]

TOSH, THOMAS, born 1794, son of Thomas Tosh and his wife Sophia Henderson, died in Calcutta on 24 November 1859. [Carnbee gravestone]

TOSHACH, ALEXANDER, schoolmaster of Culross, a deed, 16... [NRS.RD4.46.928]

TOUGH, JAMES, in Ground of Balmerino in 1717. [BA.634]

TRAILL, JOHN, of Blebo, and Catherine Ramsay, relict of Sir David Lindsay of Rathillet, a bond, 1604. [NRS.GD7.sec.1/26]

TRAILL, ROBERT, a miller in St Andrews, was admitted as a burgess of St Andrews on 8 January 1771. [SABR]

TRAILL, THOMAS, born 1720, settled in Dominica, died in July 1763. [St Andrews gravestone]

TRAIL, THOMAS, a meal-maker in St Andrews, was admitted as a burgess of St Andrews on 4 March 1755. [SABR]

TRAILL, WILLIAM, in Dominica, son of John Traill late tenant farmer in Strathkinness, Fife, and his first wife Isabel Stewart, a deed, 28 November 1793. [NRS.SC20.36.16]

TULLICE, DAVID, in the Ground of Nachtane in 1717. [BA.635]

167

TULLOS, JAMES, was admitted as a weaver burgess of Cupar on 29 September 1795. [CBR]

TURNBULL, DAVID, son of David Turnbull, [1720-1788], and his wife Janet Whyte, [1731-1784], died in Jamaica. [Dunfermline gravestone]

TURNBULL, GRIZEL, relict of William Chrystal a feuar at Torry, will, 1785. [NRS.B12.5.4/15-18]

VEATCH, ALEXANDER, a writer in Dunfermline, and his wife Katharine Adie, a heritable bond, 1749. [NRS.RD3.211/2.13]

VEITCH, JANET, only child of Alexander Veitch a merchant in Dunfermline, 1769. [NRS.CS16.1.134]

VEITCH, WILLIAM, a merchant in Dunfermline, 1769. [NRS.CS16.1.134]

VILANT, WILLIAM, of Pinkerton, Professor of Civil History, University of St Andrews, a deed, 1751. [NRS.RD4.178/1.373]

VILANT, WILLIAM, a meal-maker in St Andrews, was admitted as a burgess of St Andrews on 18 November 1761. [SABR]

WADDELL, ROBERT, a ship's carpenter in Cellardyke, a deed,1752. [NRS.RD3.211/2.131]

WAID, JOHN, a baker in Elie, and his wife Janet Findlay, a deed, 1656. [NRS.GD1.27.8]

WALKER, ALEXANDER, son of Livingstone Walker and his wife Mary Ballingall, a shipbuilder in Grenada before 1810. [Dunino gravestone]

WALKER, ANDREW, MA, minister at Auchtertool from 1652 until 1665. [F.V.78]

WALKER, ANDREW, a tailor in St Andrews, was admitted as a burgess of St Andrews on 2 February 1765. [SABR]

WALKER, DAVID, schoolmaster of Collessie, 1669, 1690. [SUL.ms36929.5.708][SHS.4.2]

WALKER, DAVID, a tanner in Leslie, a deed, 1752. [NRS.RD4.178/2.331]

WALKER, DAVID, only son of William Walker a merchant and guilds-brother of St Andrews, was admitted as a burgess of St Andrews on 22 December 1769. [SABR]

WALKER, GEORGE, in St Andrews, was admitted as a burgess of St Andrews on 8 November 1770. [SABR]

WALKER, GEORGE, in Cupar, was admitted as a burgess of St Andrews in 1774. [SABR]

WALKER, ISOBEL, born 1771, daughter of Reverend William Walker and his wife Margaret Manderston in Collessie, died 1853 in Jamaica. [F.5.135]

WALKER, JAMES, a flax-dresser, son-in-law of James Wilson the town clerk, was admitted as a burgess of Dunfermline on 17 August 1792. [DM]

WALKER, JOHN, master of the Jean of Leven in Veere, Zealand, in 1736. [NRS.RH11/2]

WALKER, JOHN, a merchant in Elie, deeds, 1752. [NRS.RD4.211/2.131, 249; RD4.178/1.80, 321, 426]

WALKER, JOHN, in Kilconquhar, was admitted as a burgess of St Andrews on 10 September 1765. [SABR]

WALKER, JOHN, a merchant in Charleston, South Carolina, was admitted as a burgess of St Andrews on 13 June 1775. [SABR]

WALKER, PETER, a weaver in Cupar, was admitted as a burgess of St Andrews in 1774. [SABR]

WALKER, ROBERT, schoolmaster of Auchterderran, a deed, 1678. [NRS.RD4.42.400]

WALKER, ROBERT, a baker in St Andrews, son of David Walker a baker, was admitted as a burgess of St Andrews on 23 January 1759. [SABR]

WALKER, SIMEON, a cook from Burntisland, aboard the Caledonia bound for Darien in 1698, testament, 1707, Comm. Edinburgh. [NRS]

WALKER, WILLIAM, a sailor in Coaltown of Durie, son of William Walker, aboard the Unicorn bound for Darien in 1698, testament, 1707, Comm. Edinburgh. [NRS]

WALKER, WILLIAM, a surgeon in Leven, was admitted as a burgess of St Andrews 19 August 1775. [SABR]

WALKER, WILLIAM, clerk of Inverkeithing, was admitted as a burgess of St Andrews on 9 September 1775. [SABR]

WALKER, WILLIAM, born 1768, daughter of Reverend William Walker and his wife Margaret Manderston in Collessie, died 1799 in Jamaica. [F.5.135]

WALLACE, ALEXANDER, in St Andrews, was admitted as a burgess of St Andrews on 29 December 1757. [SABR]

WALLACE, DAVID, a wright in Kilrenny, was admitted as a burgess of St Andrews on 29 September 1755. [SABR]

WALLACE, DAVID, born 21 August 1791 in Pittenweem, husband of Helen ...., formerly residing in Calcutta, died in Pittenweem on 17 December 1839. [Pittenweem gravestone]

WALLACE, GEORGE, shore-master in Dysart, a deed, 1752. [NRS.RD3.211/2.501]

WALLACE, LAURENCE, in St Andrews, was admitted as a burgess of St Andrews on 8 September 1775. [SABR]

WALLACE, RACHEL, widow of John Thomson a wright in Wemyss, a deed, 1752. [NRS.RD2.172.37]

WALLACE, THOMAS, born 1794, son of Willian and Esther Wallace, died in the Amazon on 12 October 1863. [St Andrews gravestone]

WALLACE, WALTER, in Kilmukis, a charter witness, 21 July 1654. [RGS.X.311]

WALLS, RICHARD, a weaver in Dunfermline, a deed, 1752. [NRS.RD3.211/2.134]

WALLWOOD, WILLIAM, was served heir to his father James Wallwood of Touch, on 2 February 1700. [NRS.Retours.Fife.1436]

WANCH, DAVID, from Kinghorn, died aboard the Friends Adventure at sea, probate, 1688. [TNA]

WANN, JAMES, in St Andrews, was admitted as a burgess of St Andrews on 20 December 1762. [SABR]

WAN, JAMES, a weaver in St Andrews, was admitted as a burgess of St Andrews on 7 September 1775. [SABR]

WARDLAW, DAVID, a clothier in Dunfermline, a deed, 1752. [NRS.RD2.172.277]

WARDLAW, JOHN, MA, minister in Dunfermline from 1679 to 1681. [F.V.29]

WARDLAW, MARGARET, daughter of Sir Henry Wardlaw of Pitrevie, and widow of James KinnInmonth of that Ilk, was confirmed in various lands in the parish of Auchterderran formerly held by her husband, on 24 June 1664. [RGS.XI.604]

WATERSTON, HENRY, a councillor of Burntisland in 1689. [RPCS.XIV.455]

WATSON, ALEXANDER, born 1795, a planter who was naturalised in 1825 in Charleston, South Carolina. [NARA.M1183/1]

WATSON, ANDREW, schoolmaster of Kennoway, 1690. [SHS.4.2]

WATSON, ANDREW, a weaver in St Andrews, was admitted as a burgess of St Andrews on 1 September 1775. [SABR]

WATSON, CHARLES, a wright and a councillor of Burntisland in 1689. [RPCS.XIV.455]

WATSON, JAMES, from Burntisland, a sailor aboard the Caledonia at Darien in 1698, testament, 1707, Comm. Edinburgh. [NRS]

WATSON, JAMES, born 1782 in Fife, a mariner who was naturalised in 1807 in Charleston, South Carolina. [NARA.M1183/1]

WATSON, JOHN, a salt officer in Dysart, deed, 1750. [NRS.RD2.171/2.83]

WATSON, KATHERINE, from Cupar, guilty of infanticide, was transported to America in 1777. [SM.38.511]

WATSON, MARY or MARJORY, daughter of Thomas Watson an innkeeper in Auchtermuchty, married Alexander a clerk in 1765, Process of Divorce in November 1778. [NRS.CC8.6.599]

WATSON, ROBERT, son of Andrew Watson and his wife Ann Hutton, died on St Vincent in 1803. [St Andrews Cathedral gravestone]

WATSON, THOMAS, son of Alexander Watson and his wife Agnes Key, died on 13 August 1802 in India. [St Andrews Cathedral gravestone]

WATSON, WILLIAM, minister at Burntisland from 1601 until 1616. [F.V.81]

WATT, ANDREW, a skipper in Burntisland, testament, 1737, Comm. Edinburgh. [NRS]

WATT, JOHN, a mariner in Limekilns, testament, 1608, Comm. Edinburgh. [NRS]

WATT, JOHN, from Cupar, married Lilian Thomson, in the Scots Kirk in Rotterdam on 9 February 1716. [GAR]

WATT, JOHN, son of John Watt overseer to Major Peter Preston of Valleyfield, apprenticed to David Cunningham a skipper in Torry for 3 years, in 1770. [NRS.B12.5.3/152-153]

WATT, THOMAS, from Auchtervale, foremast-man aboard the Caledonia, died at Darien, Panama,1696, testament, 1707. Comm. Edinburgh. [NRS]

WEDDERBURN, ALEXANDER, of Wedderburn and Birkhill, born 1742, died 4 July 1811, his wife Elizabeth Ferguson died on 13 October 1810. [Balmerino gravestone]

WEDDERBURN, HENRY, of Wedderburn and Birkhill, born 3 November 1755, died 30 December 1841, husband of Mary Turner Maitland, born 24 October 1768, died 21 October 1851. [Balmerino gravestone]

WEEMS, JAMES, the elder, of Pitkinnie, a Jacobite, was arrested and taken bound for Edinburgh via Kirkcaldy where his son James Weems the younger, his brother David Weems, Andrew

Balcanquell in Kirkcaldy, and Patrick Murray a sea-waiter there, forcibly liberated him, 1689. [RPCS.XIV.515]

WEDDERBURN, JAMES, emigrated to South Carolina in 1733, Clerk to the Common Pleas there, received land grants in 1737-1738. [CSPAWI]

WEEMS, JOHN, was served heir to his father Ronald Weems of Lathoker on 23 July 1691. [NRS.Retours.Fife.1318]

WEIR, GAVIN, a preacher in Newbigging of Carnock, a bond, 1751. [NRS.RD2.172.428]

WEMYSS, ALEXANDER, a skipper in Aberdour, a contract, 1751. [NRS.RD4.178/2.97]

WEMYSS, JAMES, born 1750, son of John Wemyss and his wife Cecilia Durie in Mains of Bogie, graduated MA from St Andrews, minister at Burntisland from 1779 until 1820, died 2 February 1822. [F.V.83]

WEMYSS, JOHN, schoolmaster of Inverkeithing, a deed, 1667. [NRS.RD4.19.564]

WEMYSS, JOHN, son of John Wemyss a joiner in St Andrews, was admitted as a burgess of St Andrews on 9 September 1773. [SABR]

WEMYSS, ROBERT, born 1796, commander of the Bombay Castle in India, died in Edinburgh on 19 February 1860. [St Andrews gravestone]

WEMYSS, THOMAS, son of David Wemyss of Foodie, graduated MA from St Andrews in 1676, Episcopalian minister of Kinkell from 1683 to 1695. [SEC.147]

WEST, JAMES, born 11 June 1791, son of John West in Kirkcaldy, emigrated to America in 1815, settled in Wood County, West Virginia, died in Fox Township, Ohio, in 1851. [OVG.125]

WHITE, ANDREW, from Cellardyke, a mariner aboard HMS Restoration, probate 1696, Prerogative Court of Canterbury. [TNA]

WHITE, ANDREW, tenant in Coultra, Balmerino, testament, 1786, Comm. St Andrews. [NRS]

WHYTE, ARCHIBALD, born 1654, a burgess, died 12 February 1724. [Culross Abbey gravestone]

WHYTE, DAVID, a maltster and brewer in Dunnikeir, a deed, 1752. [NRS.RD4.178/1.451]

WHYTE, ELIZABETH, born 1754, a servant at Arnot's Mill, emigrated to Philadelphia aboard the Friendship in 1775. [TNA.T47.12]

WHITE, GEORGE, born 30 June 1701 in Carmichael, tenant in Hattonhill, died 1 September 1784. [Abdie gravestone]

WHYTE, HENDRY, a councillor of Burntisland in 1689. [RPCS.XIV.455]

WHYTE, HENRY, a burgess of Newburgh by 1740. [NBR]

WHYTE, JAMES, born 1777 in Kirkcaldy, emigrated via Liverpool to America, a merchant intending to settle in Mississippi, naturalised in New York on 6 January 1819.

WHYTE, JOHN, master of the Happy Betty of Kirkcaldy trading with Virginia in 1766. [NRS.E504.3.3]

WHITE, ROBERT, minister at Ferry-Port-on-Craig, a bond, 18 July 1690. [NRS.GD137.3083]

WHITE, WILLIAM, schoolmaster of Kinkell, a deed, 1679. [NRS.RD4.44.319]

WIGHTMAN, CHARLES, son of Charles Wightman in Anstruther, a merchant in Tobago in 1778. [NRS.CS16.1.174]

WIGHTON, HENRY, from Kirkcaldy, a foremastman aboard the Caledonia at Darien in 1698, testament, 1707, Comm. Edinburgh. [NRS]

WILKIE, ALEXANDER, in St Andrews, was admitted as a burgess of St Andrews on 3 September 1763. [SABR]

WILKIE, JOHN, born 1638, son of Harry Wilkie in Wemyss, graduated MA from St Andrews in 1658, minister at Auchtertool in 1665, died 18 March 1665. [F.V.78]

WILKIE, JOHN, master of the Industry of Dysart trading with Bremen in 1762. [NRS.E504.3.3]

WILKIE, WILLIAM, born 1740, died 24 March 1811. [Abdie gravestone]

WILLIAMSON, ALEXANDER, a burgess of Newburgh by 1740. [NBR]

WILLIAMSON, ANDREW, from Largo, applied to become a burgess of Bergen, Norway, in 1641. [SAB]

WILLIAMSON, DAVID, master of the Anna of Elie trading with Danzig in 1683. [NRS.E72.9.15]

WILLIAMSON, JAMES, schoolmaster of Aberdour, husband of Barbara Stevenson, a deed, 1685. [NRS.RD3.61.243]

WILLIAMSON, JAMES, born 1642, son of David Williamson a schoolmaster in Cupar, graduated MA from St Andrews in 1662, Episcopalian minister at Cameron from 1668 to 1677, and Kirkcaldy from 1677 to 1689, died 4 August 1728. [SEC.148]

WILLIAMSON, JAMES, master of the Friendship of Leven trading with Norway in 1719. [NRS.CE52.1.3]

WILLIAMSON, JOHN, schoolmaster of Cupar Grammar School, husband of Bessie Honeyman, deeds, 1680-1701.[SHS.4.2] [NRS.RD2.52.189; RD4.63.80; RD3.61.358; RD2.85.139]

WILLIAMSON, JOHN, master of the Marie of Pittenweem trading between Pittenweem and Bruges, Flanders, in 1684. [NRS.E72.9.17]

WILLIAMSON, JOHN, a sailor in Cardenden, son of James Williamson, aboard the Unicorn bound for Darien in 1698, testament, 1707, Comm. Edinburgh. [NRS]

WILLIAMSON, MAGNUS, from Kirkcaldy, a burgess of Bergen, Norway, in 1619. [SAB]

WILLIAMSON, ROBERT, schoolmaster of Cupar, husband of [1] Margaret Glasford, [2] Bessie Boustoun, sasine, 1625, [NRS.RS30.6.81]; deeds, 1661-1662, [NRS.RD3.1.19; RD4.5.468]

WILLIAMSON, ROBERT, schoolmaster of Elie, 1690. [SHS.4.2]

WILLIAMSON. THOMAS, mariner and co-owner of the Balcomie of Kinghorn, testament, 1803, Comm. St Andrews. [NRS]

WILSON, ALEXANDER, in Freirton, born 1562, died 3 May 1636, husband of Christian Smyth, born 1570, died 25 March 1638. [Burntisland, St Columba's, gravestone]

WILSON, ALEXANDER, son of Thomas Wilson a merchant in Kinghorn, was apprenticed to James Ker a goldsmith in Edinburgh for seven years, on 18 March 1761. [ERA]

WILSON, CHARLES, a ship's mate in Coaltown of Balgonie, aboard the Olive Branch bound for Darien in 1698, testament, 1707, Comm. Edinburgh. [NRS]

WILSON, DAVID, a sailor in Wemyss, aboard the Caledonia bound for Darien in 1698, testament, 1707, Comm. Edinburgh. [NRS]

WILSON, DAVID, born 1794, son of David Wilson and his wife Margaret Duncan, died 1815 in Calcutta, India. [Carnbee gravestone]

WILSON, GEORGE, a sailor in Dysart, son of James Wilson and his wife Margaret McEwan, aboard the Rising Sun bound for Darien in 1699, testament, 1707, Comm. Edinburgh. [NRS]

WILSN, GEORGE, in St Andrews, was admitted as a burgess of St Andrews on 28 February 1756. [SABR]

WILSON, GILBERT, formerly a burgess of Pitterco in Poland, a sasine in Fife, 20 February 1621. [NRS.RS1.7.213]

WILSON, JAMES, a brewer in Falkland, and his daughters Mary and Margaret, a deed. 1746. [NRS.CS228.B3.40]

WILSON, JAMES, the town clerk of Dunfermline, was admitted as a burgess of St Andrews on 31 July 1760. [SABR]

WILSON, JAMES, a merchant burgess of Cupar, was admitted as a burgess of St Andrews on 8 November 1770. [SABR]

WILSON, JAMES, born 1768, son of Walter Wilson, a Major in the Service of the Honorable East India Company, died in Bangalore, India. [St Andrews gravestone]

WILSON, JOHN, a boatswain in Coaltown of Balgonie, aboard the Dolphin bound for Darien in 1698, testament, 1708, Comm. Edinburgh. [NRS]

WILSON, JOHN, a writer in St Andrews, a deed, 1751. [NRS.RD2.171/2.359]

WILSON, JOHN, a meal-maker in St Andrews, was admitted as a burgess of St Andrews on 13 November 1755. [SABR]

WILSON, JOHN, a baker from Fife who settled in New York in 1778, died at sea aboard the brig Peace between Jamaica and New York on 19 August 1809. [ANY.I.225]

WILSON, MUNGO, in St Andrews, was admitted as a burgess of St Andrews on 30 May 1758. [SABR]

WILSON, ROBERT, an apothecary and surgeon in Burntisland, emigrated to South Carolina in 1753. [CLRO/AIA]

WILSON, ROBERT, a writer in Dunfermline, was admitted as a burgess of St Andrews on 31 July 1760. [SABR]

WILSON, THOMAS, son of Walter Wilson, a Lieutenant in the Service of the Honorable East India Company, died 10 May 1759 in India. [St Andrews Cathedral gravestone]

WILSON, THOMAS, a merchant in Kemback, was admitted as a burgess of St Andrews on 15 December 1757. [SABR]

WILSON, THOMAS, born in 1779, son of Dr Charles Wilson and his wife Elizabeth Stark, a Lieutenant General in the Service of the Honorable East India Company, in April 1856 in Wales. [St Andrews gravestone]

WILSON, WILLIAM, son of Andrew Wilson of Enderdivett, graduated MA from St Andrews in 1658, Episcopalian minister in Cupar from 1665 to 1689. [SEC.149]

WILSON, WILLIAM, in St Andrews, was admitted as a burgess of St Andrews on 3 January 1762. [SABR]

WILSON, WILLIAM, son of William Wilson in Buckhaven, and Janet Grant from Aberdeenshire, were married in the Scots Kirk in Rotterdam on 5 March 1778. [GAR]

WILSON, WILLIAM, a sailor in St Monance, husband of Susannah Duncan, a sasine, 1783. [NRS.RS.Fife.566]

WINRAM, KATHERINE, daughter of John Winram a dyer in Kirkcaldy, a marriage contract, 1737. [NRS.RD2.171/2.378]

WINTON, JAMES, in Birchill, Balmerino, 1717. [BA.634]

WINTON, JOHN, a burgess of Newburgh by 1740. [NBR]

WINTON, WILLIAM, a burgess of Newburgh by 1740. [NBR]

WISHART, JOHN, in St Andrews, was admitted as a burgess of St Andrews on 1 September 1775. [SABR]

WISHART, MARGARET, in Ferry-Port-on-Craig, 1762. [NRS.CH2.150.4.29]

WISHART, WILLIAM, a sailor in Burntisland, testament, 1805, Comm. St Andrews. [NRS]

WITHERSPOON, WILLIAM, a maltman burgess of Culross, a deed, 1761. [NRS.B12.5.2/249-257]

WOOD, ALEXANDER, of Elie, was admitted as a burgess of St Andrews on 9 February 1771. [SABR]

WOOD, CHRISTINE, spouse of William Wemyss an advocate and bailie of St Andrews, sasines, 1607/1608. [NRS.RS30.X.64; XI.162/203/224]

WOOD, JAMES, master of the Jean of Pittenweem trading with Danzig in 1748. [NRS.E504.27.1.2]

WOOD, JOHN, son of Andrew Wood of Largo, a sasine, 1608. [NRS.RS30.XI.58]

WOOD, JOHN, MA, born 1651, son of Provost James Wood of St Andrews, Episcopalian minister of St Andrews from 1686 unti 1689, died in June 1703. [SEC.150]

WOOD, WILLIAM, born 1651, graduated MA from St Andrews in 1671, Episcopalian minister of Dunino from 1683 to 1693, died in April 1693. [SEC.150]

WOOD, WILLIAM, born in 1766, a fisherman in Cellardyke, died on 23 February 1820. [Kilrenny gravestone]

WOODCOCK, ALEXANDER, a mariner in Crail, grandson and heir of James Woodcock a weaver in Crail, and Isabel Wallace, 1764. [NRS.B10.5.1/48]

WYLD, JOHN, in Milton of Borland, a sasine, 1603. [NRS.RS30.IV.246]

WYLLE, JOHN, born 1613, schoolmaster of Balmerino, died 7 December 1705. [Balmerino gravestone]

WYLLIE, AGNES, relict of Alexander Normand a gardener in St Andrews, afterwards spouse to John Goudie a gardener there, testament, 1752, Comm. St Andrews. [NRS]

WYLLIE, JAMES, cook and gardener of New College, St Andrews, a bond, 1759. [NRS.B65.4/325]

WYLLIE, JOHN, of Leadwells of Balmerino, 1694; a tack in 1700. [NRS.SC20.33.7/142][BA.632]

YAIR, ELIZABETH, spouse of Stephen Laing, portioner of Auchtermuchty, sasines, 1603, 1604. [NRS.RS30.IV.176; VII.191]

YOOL, JAMES, a skipper in St Andrews, a deed, 1726. [NRS.B65.5.3/9]

YOULL, DAVID, a mariner in St Andrews in 1708. [NRS.B65.8.4]

YOUNG, AGNES, mother of Simon Milne a burgess of Pittenweem, a sasine, 1604. [NRS.RS30.V.149]

YOUNG, ALEXANDER, graduated MA at Edinburgh University in 1681, Episcopalian minister in Culross from 1684 to 1697. [SEC.152]

YOUNG, ALEXANDER, from Fife, was naturalised in Camden, South Carolina, in 1806. [South Carolina Citizenship Book.54] [South Carolina Archives, Miscellaneous Records, volume 8]

YOUNG, DAVID, a land laborer in St Andrews, testament, 1751, Comm. St Andrews. [NRS]

YOUNG, DAVID, was admitted as an inn-keeper burgess of Crail in 1800. [CBR]

YOUNG, GEORGE, a messenger in St Andrews, bonds, 1707, 1711. [NRS.B66.5.5/44, 130]

YOUNG, JAMES, a foremast-man in Abbotshall, aboard the Caledonia bound for Darien in 1698, testament, 1707, Comm. Edinburgh. [NRS]

YOUNG, JAMES, born 1731, died 1704, husband of Janet Collier, born 1736, died 1785. [Burntisland, St Columba's gravestone]

YOUNG, JOHN, master of the Seaflower of Dysart trading with Hamburg in 1767. [NRS.E504.3.3]

YOUNG, JOHN, son of James Young in St Andrews, was admitted as a burgess of St Andrews on 6 December 1755. [SABR]

YOUNG, JOHN, born 1760, son of John Young, a mariner, died on 23 May 1783. [Ferry Port on Craig gravestone]

YOUNG, MATTHEW, born 1708, died 11 November 1783, husband of Margaret Oliphant, born 1734, died 17 February 1817. [Burntisland, St Columba's, gravestone]

YOUNG, MAURICE, son of Reverend John Young, was admitted as a burgess of St Andrews on 6 March 1758. [SABR]

YOUNG, ROBERT, a tenant in Kirkton of Forgan, letters of poinding, 17 August 1680. [NRS.NRAS.3215, Largo papers]

YOUNG, THOMAS, an Episcopalian priest in Falkland, a letter, 1740. [NRS.CH12.12.1091]

YOUNG, THOMAS, master of the Newcastle Packet of Crail 1742. [NRS.E504.3.1]; master of the Margaret of Leven trading with Norway and Rotterdam in 1744. [NRS.E504.27.1]

YOUNG, THOMAS, a skipper in Kinghorn, testament, 1757, Comm. Edinburgh. [NRS]

YOUNG, WILLIAM, Provost of St Salvador's College, St Andrews, testament, 1747, Comm. St Andrews. [NRS]

YOUNG, WILLIAM, a sheep-stealer in Kelty, was transported to the colonies in 1774. [AJ.1377]

YOUNG, Captain, a shipmaster of Burntisland, bound for Virginia in 1716. [NRS.AC8.199]

YOUNGSON, WILLIAM, schoolmaster of Carnbie, 1690. [SHS.4.2]

YUILL. JOHN, a tailor in Milton of Balgonie, husband of Eupham Lawson, a sasine, 1608. [NRS.RS30.XI.40]

YUIL, ROBERT, a shipmaster in St Andrews, died 2 July 1635. [St Andrews gravestone]

YUILL, ROBERT, a maltman in Dysart, husband of Christian Black, sasines, 1603, 1607. [NRS.RS30.IV.72/146; RS30.X.165]